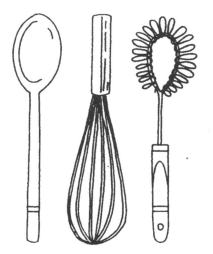

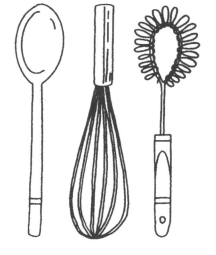

The Ultimate
30 minute
COOKBOOK

The Ultimate
30 minute
COOKBOOK

BARNES
&NOBLE
BOOKS
NEW YORK

This edition published by Barnes & Noble, Inc.,
by arrangement with Anness Publishing Limited

2003 Barnes & Noble Books

M 10 9 8 7 6 5 4 3 2

ISBN 0 7607 4854 3

©Anness Publishing Limited 1998, 1999, 2001, 2003
Hermes House
88-89 Blackfriars Road
London SE1 8HA

A CIP catalogue record for this book is available from the British Library

Publisher: Joanna Lorenz
Senior Editor: Linda Fraser
Designer: Ian Sandom
Jacket Design: Lisa Tai
Indexer: Hilary Bird
Photography: Karl Adamson, Steve Baxter, William Lingwood, Patrick McLeavy and Tom Odulate
Recipes: Alex Barker, Kit Chan, Christine France, Sarah Gates, Shirley Gill, Soheila Kimberley,
Elizabeth Lambert Ortiz, Maggie Pannell and Hilaire Walden

Printed and bound in Singapore

CONTENTS

Introduction *6*

Quick-Cooking Techniques *8*

Mix and Match Menus *10*

INTRODUCTION

Today's hectic lifestyle means that most people have less and less time to spend in the kitchen. After a hard day, either at work or at home, few of us feel inclined to spend hours slaving over a hot stove—or even a microwave oven. Paradoxically, however, we do all want interesting, well-presented, healthy meals that are colorful and full of flavor.

So what's the solution? Do you pop into the nearest supermarket and stock up on those expensive prepared meals, or do you build up a repertoire of fast, easy dishes that can be made in the brief moments between getting home from work or returning from the school run and rushing out again?

That's where we come in. For this book, we've assembled as fine a collection of quick-cook recipes as you could find anywhere. For the ultimate fast food, turn to those in the first section that take less than ten minutes. Even the longest recipe in this book can be completed in half an hour—and you can't beat that.

Of course, precisely how long each dish will actually take depends on a number of factors: the competence of the cook; the distractions (children, pets, partners); and how many glasses of wine are consumed in the process. Some dishes benefit from being chilled or marinated if time permits, but when time is short, simply skip these options.

Preparation and cooking times for each recipe are given as a guide. Where these are inextricably linked, as when the cook puts on a pot of pasta, then uses the time it cooks to prepare the vegetables for a sauce, a single time is given.

Master a few favorite recipes and you're ready for the next challenge—the thirty-minute menu! Some suggestions for mix-and-match dishes are given in the pages that follow, together with techniques for basic recipes that are infinitely adaptable.

QUICK-COOK SHORTCUTS
The canny cook cheats. Digging your own potatoes or picking and shelling your own peas are both admirable pursuits, and the results are doubtless delicious, but for fabulous fast food what you really need is a first-class supermarket that will do the hard work for you. It is now possible to buy a huge range of vegetables and fruits that are ready to cook, from trimmed green beans and snow peas to carrot sticks and sliced onions.

Most types of fruit are easy enough to prepare, but look for sliced fresh pineapple, mango and melon—fresh and tasty, without any fuss.

Salad greens are available in astonishing variety—not cheap, but wonderfully convenient for the quick cook—and there's an equally wide range of prepared dressings, if you can't spare a few minutes to make one of your own.

If it's medleys you're after, you'll find them, too. Packages of prepared mixed vegetables are widely available, and where once you would be lucky to find

Left: Quick-cook savory staples include flour, dried beans, bottled and canned capers, tomatoes and vegetables, fresh fruit and vegetables, wine, oils and vinegars, garlic, fresh herbs and eggs.

a single stir-fry mix there are now Thai, Chinese and other Asian mixtures. The stir-fry vegetables may even come with a sauce, so for a quick main course, all you need to do is stock up with strips of chicken breast, pork fillet or sirloin steak.

Of course, if cooking is reduced to putting together assorted packages, it isn't very satisfying. The trick is to add extra ingredients of your own to give the dish a unique signature. Herbs, spices, sauces and flavorings like fresh ginger root can make the difference between a dish that tastes like it came off an assembly line and one that has everyone begging for the recipe.

If meat is to be cooked very quickly, it must be very tender. Turkey scallops are ideal, especially if they are pounded out, then crumbed or simply cooked in a tasty sauce. Calf's liver is equally appropriate, and has the added advantage of being a good source of iron.

Fish is the original fast food: Skinned fillets need no preparation and cook extremely quickly, as does shellfish. The well-stocked pantry should include cans of tuna, anchovies and salmon—all staples that can be used to create quick meals.

So—next stop, the grocery section. Even here, there has been a revolution. Once upon a time, canned tomatoes meant whole tomatoes in a thin, seed-filled liquid. Today, the tomatoes

Right: Pantry essentials for desserts include sugar, cocoa, chocolate sauce, meringues, fresh fruit, cookies, nuts, bottled and canned fruits, and eggs.

are frequently chopped, and you can get them with herbs, garlic, chopped peppers and chiles. Passata (strained tomatoes) and puréed tomatoes, are sold in jars or cans, and tubes of tomato paste or garlic paste, are equally useful.

Also invaluable are cans or jars of fruit, pimientos, chiles, artichoke hearts, beans and peas, pesto and tapenade. Of course, these ingredients cost a little more, but convenience doesn't come without a price.

From the cold section, you'll need eggs, cream, yogurt, cheeses, butter and margarine, and pastry.

What else? Obviously, you'll need all the staples like flour, sugar, rising agents and rice. Ladyfingers, amaretti biscuits, and slabs of gingerbread are first steps to simple desserts, and pre-

pared pizza crusts and tortillas save time and effort.

When it comes to pasta, buy the fresh product if possible, as it not only tastes superb but also cooks in just a few minutes. Dried pasta that cooks in under ten minutes is also widely available, in small cuts and strings.

This book is very much in line with modern trends in cooking. We've had the prepared food revolution, and while these dishes remain a mainstay for many busy families, there has been a swing back to "real" food. We may have neither the time nor the inclination to spend hours on complicated cooking procedures, but we still want to watch food cooking, relish the aromas, hear the meat sizzle in the pan. This collection of recipes promises all that—and in next to no time.

QUICK-COOKING TECHNIQUES

Every quick cook needs a few basics that can be mixed and matched to make a meal in moments. In the savory stakes, the prime candidate has to be homemade tomato sauce. Use it to top pasta or a scone pizza; mix it with sliced smoked sausages; spoon it over grilled steaks or chicken breasts; spice it up with chiles, then serve it topped with a fried egg or pour it over cauliflower, broccoli or beans, top with grated cheese and broil until golden.

QUICK SCONE PIZZA

Preparation time 10 minutes
Cooking time 20 minutes

SERVES 4–6
1 cup self-rising white flour
1 cup whole-wheat flour
1½ teaspoons baking powder
pinch of salt
4 tablespoons butter, diced
about ⅔ cup milk
1 quantity of Tomato Sauce (see recipe at right)
toppings of your choice

1. Preheat the oven to 425°F. Mix the flours, baking powder and salt in a bowl. Rub in the butter. Add the milk and mix to a dough.

2. Knead the dough gently until smooth, then roll it out and line a 12 x 7-inch jelly roll pan, pushing up the edges to form a rim. Spread with the tomato sauce and add your favorite toppings. Bake for about 20 minutes.

TOMATO SAUCE

Preparation time 10 minutes
Cooking time 20 minutes

MAKES ABOUT 1¼ CUPS
1 tablespoon olive oil
1 onion, finely chopped
1 garlic clove, crushed
14-ounce can chopped tomatoes
1 tablespoon tomato paste
1 tablespoon chopped fresh mixed herbs
pinch of sugar
salt and ground black pepper

1. Heat the oil in a pan, add the onion and garlic and sauté over gentle heat for 5 minutes, stirring occasionally, until softened.

2. Add the tomatoes, then stir in the tomato paste, fresh mixed herbs, sugar and salt and ground black pepper to taste.

3. Bring to a boil, then simmer, uncovered, over medium heat for about 15 minutes, stirring occasionally, until the mixture has reduced to a thick pulp. Let cool, then cover the sauce and chill until ready to use.

COOKING PASTA

Preparation time None
Cooking time 3–12 minutes

SERVES 4
12 ounces pasta
salt
2 tablespoons olive oil or a pat of butter, to serve

1. Bring a large pot of lightly salted water to a boil. Add the pasta and stir to separate the strings or small cuts.

2. Cook at a rolling boil until the pasta is tender but still firm to the bite. When halved, the small cuts must be cooked through.

3. Drain the pasta well in a colander, shaking it hard to remove the excess water. Pour into a bowl and add a drizzle of olive oil or a pat of butter and then sprinkle on a little grated Parmesan or add your favorite sauce.

COOK'S TIP
Always cook pasta in plenty of water in a large pan to prevent it from sticking.

Three more great basics: Pancakes can be served simply, with lemon and sugar, but are even tastier with homemade chocolate sauce or raspberry purée, either of which can also be used to top ice cream, meringues or fruit. Raspberry purée is also delicious spooned over slices of brioche that have been soaked in egg and cream, then fried in butter.

PERFECT PANCAKES

Preparation time 5 minutes
Cooking time 20 minutes

MAKES ABOUT 12
1½ cups all-purpose flour
2 teaspoons sugar
2 eggs
1¾ cups milk
2 tablespoons butter, melted

1 Sift the flour into a bowl and stir in the sugar. Make a well in the center and add the eggs and half the milk. Stir, gradually incorporating the dry ingredients, until smooth, then beat in the remaining milk.

2 Stir most of the melted butter into the batter. Heat a crêpe pan, then grease it lightly with butter. Spoon in about ¼ cup of the batter, tilting the pan so it coats the bottom evenly. Cook until the pancake has set and small holes appear on the surface. Lift the edge; the bottom should be pale brown. Flip the pancake over. Cook the other side briefly. Slide out and keep hot while cooking more pancakes.

CHOCOLATE SAUCE

Preparation time 1 minute
Cooking time 5 minutes

MAKES 1 CUP
⅔ cup light cream
1 tablespoon sugar
5 ounces best quality semisweet chocolate, broken
2 tablespoons dark rum or whiskey (optional)

1 Rinse out a small saucepan with cold water. This will help to prevent the sauce from sticking on the bottom of the pan. Pour in the cream, stir in the sugar and bring to a boil over medium heat.

2 Remove the pan from the heat and add the chocolate, a few pieces at a time, stirring after each addition until the chocolate has melted and the sauce is smooth. Stir in the rum or whiskey, if using.

3 Pour the chocolate sauce into a pitcher and use immediately. Alternatively, pour the sauce into a clean jar and let cool. Close the jar and store the sauce in the refrigerator for up to 10 days. Serve hot or cold.

RASPBERRY PURÉE

Preparation time 1–2 minutes
Cooking time 1–5 minutes

1 Hull, clean and dry fresh raspberries and place them in a blender or food processor. Pulse the machine a few times, scraping down the sides of the bowl once or twice, until the berries form a purée.

2 If using frozen raspberries, put them in a saucepan with a little sugar and place over gentle heat to soften and release the juices. Simmer for 5 minutes, then let cool.

3 Press the purée through a fine-mesh sieve to remove any fibers or seeds. Sweeten with a little confectioners' sugar and sharpen the flavor with lemon juice or a fruit-flavored liqueur, to taste.

COOK'S TIP
Other soft summer fruits can be used to make a purée. Try strawberries or blueberries, which can be puréed raw, or peaches, apricots or nectarines, which should first be poached lightly.

MIX AND MATCH MENUS

You can produce an entire meal in less than half an hour if you mix and match carefully. Choose one dish that needs to stand or can be left to cook for at least ten minutes, during which time you can put together an appetizer, salad or speedy dessert. These flexible menus include recipes from the book and some simple ideas for which no recipe is needed.

TEENAGERS' TREAT

Guacamole can be made in moments and is delicious with either spicy tortilla chips or crisp vegetable crudités.

Save time and effort by getting each guest to top his or her own Pita Pizza.

Instant salad: Mix bought washed mixed salad greens with sliced avocado, red onion, orange segments and walnuts.

Ice Cream Strawberry Shortcake is a quick and simple assembly job that is best done at the last minute.

FAMILY FAVORITE

Fresh Tomato Soup needs to simmer for 10 minutes, during which time you can prepare the burgers and make the dessert.

Beef and Mushroom Burgers make a tasty main course. Prepare the salad while they cook.

Chopped salad vegetables with crumbled feta cheese and olives make Persian Salad a flavorful accompaniment. Add the dressing at the last minute.

For a final flourish, serve Baked Peaches with a Cornflake topping with cream or vanilla ice cream.

SOPHISTICATED SUPPER

Sautéed Scallops are very quick and easy, so cook them at the very last minute.

Panfried Veal Chops is a good main course; make the sauce while cooking the appetizer.

As an accompaniment, serve crusty bread or rolls and Citrus-Green Leaf Salad, omitting the croutons if time is very short.

There's no time to make an elaborate dessert, so simply serve fresh raspberries or strawberries and some heavy cream.

VEGETARIAN FEAST

Make an easy appetizer by serving warm focaccia bread with sea salt crystals and olives.

Leek and Caraway Gratin with a Carrot Crust can easily be baked alongside the tomatoes.

Garlic Baked Tomatoes bring color to the menu and taste absolutely delicious—if you like, substitute halved cherry tomatoes for the larger tomatoes and cut the cooking time by about half.

Finally, assemble Figs with Ricotta Cream while the main-course casseroles are in the oven.

PARTY TIME

Quick suggestions for party food: Serve Hummus with pita bread instead of toast.

Tomato and Mozzarella Toasts resemble mini-pizzas and are perfect for parties.

Smoked Mackerel and Apple Dip is another quick and easy appetizer. Serve it with crisp breadsticks, fingers of hot toast or colorful vegetable crudités.

Make miniature Asparagus Rolls and serve with butter sauce or a mayonnaise dip.

LIGHT LUNCH

Melon and Grapefruit Cocktail is a cool and refreshing first course without being filling.

Crunchy-topped Cod is a good light main course, and needs very little attention during cooking.

While the cod is cooking, toss together Mixed Vegetables with Aromatic Seeds to serve as a tasty accompaniment.

Brazilian Coffee Bananas is one of the easiest desserts in the book. Make it just before serving.

10-MINUTE RECIPES

If you only have ten minutes to spare, take the fast track. Simple soups like Avgolemono get you off to a racing start, as do appetizers like Smoked Trout Salad or Prosciutto with Mango. Take a tip from the tapas table and try Garlic Shrimp or Chorizo in Olive Oil. Want something substantial as well as speedy? Pork with Camembert fits the bill. Finally, as you roar into the homestretch, Chocolate Fudge Sundaes or Brazilian Coffee Bananas will have everyone cheering.

AVGOLEMONO

This is the most popular of Greek soups. The name means "egg and lemon," the two important ingredients, which produce a light, nourishing soup. Orzo is rice-shaped, Greek pasta, but you can use any small pasta cuts.

Preparation time 2 minutes
Cooking time 5 minutes

SERVES 4–6
7½ cups chicken stock
1 cup orzo pasta
3 eggs
juice of 1 large lemon
salt and ground black pepper
lemon slices, to garnish

1 | Pour the stock into a large pan, and bring to a boil. Add the pasta and cook for 5 minutes.

2 | Beat the eggs until frothy, then add the lemon juice and 1 tablespoon of cold water. Slowly stir in a ladleful of the hot chicken stock, then add one or two more. Return this mixture to the pan, off the heat, and stir well. Season with salt and pepper and serve at once, garnished with lemon slices. Do not let the soup boil once the eggs have been added, or it will curdle.

COOK'S TIPS
Good-quality chicken stock is the secret of this speedy recipe. Look for cartons of stock in the refrigerator section of your local supermarket, or buy low-salt canned bouillon.

Making your own stock may sound like a chore, but if you recycle the meaty carcass of a roast chicken, it can be prepared in less time than it takes to clear the table after dinner.

Just pop the carcass in a pan, add an onion, a carrot and a bouquet garni, pour in water to cover generously and bring it to a boil. Lower the heat to the lowest setting, cover the pan and let the stock simmer for about 2 hours, or until the aroma reminds you that it is time to turn it off.

Strain the stock into a bowl, cool it quickly, then skim off any fat from the surface. Chicken stock freezes well for up to 3 months and should be seasoned on thawing.

THAI-STYLE CORN SOUP

This is a very quick and easy soup. If you are using frozen shrimp, thaw them before adding them to the soup.

Preparation time 3 minutes
Cooking time 5 minutes

SERVES 4

½ teaspoon safflower or sunflower oil
2 scallions, thinly sliced
1 garlic clove, crushed
2½ cups chicken stock
15-ounce can creamed corn
1¼ cups cooked, peeled shrimp
1 teaspoon green chile paste or chili
  sauce (optional)
salt and ground black pepper
cilantro leaves, to garnish

1 Heat the oil in a large, heavy saucepan and sauté the scallions and garlic over medium heat until softened.

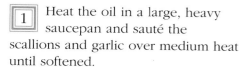

2 Stir in the chicken stock, creamed corn, shrimp and chile paste or sauce, if using.

3 Bring the soup to a boil, stirring occasionally. Season with salt and ground black pepper to taste, then serve at once, sprinkling with cilantro leaves to garnish.

COOK'S TIP
If creamed corn is not available, use ordinary canned corn, puréed in a food processor for a few seconds, until the mixture is creamy yet retains some texture.

VARIATIONS
To make Thai-style Crab and Corn Soup, use canned or freshly cooked crab in place of all or some of the cooked, peeled shrimp.

PANFRIED CHICKEN LIVER SALAD

This Florentine salad uses vin santo, a delicious sweet dessert wine from Tuscany, but this is not essential— any dessert wine will do, or a sweet or cream sherry.

Preparation time 4 minutes
Cooking time 6 minutes

SERVES 4

3 ounces fresh baby spinach leaves
3 ounces lollo rossa leaves
5 tablespoons olive oil
1 tablespoon butter
8 ounces chicken livers, trimmed and thinly sliced
3 tablespoons vin santo
2–3 ounces fresh Parmesan cheese, shaved into curls
salt and ground black pepper

1 Wash and dry the spinach and lollo rossa. Tear the leaves into a large bowl, season with salt and ground black pepper to taste and toss gently to mix.

2 Heat 2 tablespoons of the oil with the butter in a large, heavy frying pan. When foaming, add the chicken livers and toss over medium to high heat for 5 minutes, or until the livers are browned on the outside but still pink in the center. Remove from the heat.

3 Remove the livers from the pan with a slotted spoon, drain them on paper towels, then place on top of the salad greens.

4 Return the pan to medium heat, add the remaining oil and the vin santo and stir until sizzling. Pour the hot dressing over the greens and livers and toss to coat. Put the salad in a serving bowl and sprinkle the Parmesan shavings over it. Serve at once.

DEEP-FRIED WHITEBAIT

The spicy coating on the fish gives this fast favorite a crunchy bite.

Preparation time 2 minutes
Cooking time 7–8 minutes

SERVES 6
1 cup all-purpose flour
½ teaspoon curry powder
½ teaspoon ground ginger
½ teaspoon ground cayenne pepper
pinch of salt
2½ pounds fresh or frozen
  whitebait, thawed
vegetable oil, for deep-frying
lemon wedges, to garnish

1 Sift the flour into a bowl and stir in the curry powder, ground ginger, cayenne and salt.

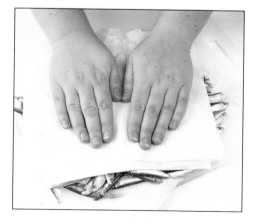

2 Lay two sheets of paper towel on the work surface. Spread out the whitebait on top, then cover with more paper towels. Blot the fish thoroughly to dry them.

3 Add a few whitebait at a time to the seasoned flour and stir gently until they are evenly coated. Heat the oil in a large, heavy saucepan until it reaches a temperature of 375°F.

4 Fry the whitebait in batches for 2–3 minutes, until the fish is golden and crispy. Drain well on paper towels, keeping each batch hot while cooking the next. Serve hot, garnished with lemon wedges.

MELON AND GRAPEFRUIT COCKTAIL

This pretty, colorful appetizer is perfect for all those occasions when you don't have much time for cooking, but want something really special to eat.

Preparation time 8 minutes
Cooking time None

SERVES 4

1 small Galia, Ogen or honeydew melon
1 small Charentais melon or cantaloupe
2 pink grapefruit
3 tablespoons orange juice
4 tablespoons red vermouth
seeds from ½ pomegranate
mint sprigs, to garnish

COOK'S TIP
To check if the melons are ripe, smell them—they should have a heady aroma, and give slightly when pressed gently at the stem end.

1 Halve the melons lengthwise and scoop out all the seeds. Cut into wedges and remove the skins, then cut across into large bite-size pieces. Set the melon aside.

2 Using a small, sharp knife, cut the peel and pith from the grapefruit. Holding the fruit over a bowl to catch the juice, cut between the grapefruit membranes to release the segments.

3 Stir the orange juice and vermouth into the reserved grapefruit juice.

4 Arrange the melon pieces and grapefruit segments on four individual serving plates. Spoon the dressing over them, then sprinkle with the pomegranate seeds. Decorate with mint sprigs.

PROSCIUTTO WITH MANGO

Other fresh, colorful fruits, such as figs, papaya or melon would go equally well with the prosciutto in this light, elegant appetizer. It is amazingly simple to prepare and can be made in advance—ideal if you are serving a complicated main course.

Preparation time 5 minutes
Cooking time None

SERVES 4

12 slices Prosciutto
1 ripe mango
ground black pepper
flat-leaf parsley sprigs, to garnish

1 Separate the prosciutto slices and arrange three on each of four individual plates, crumpling the prosciutto slightly to give a decorative effect.

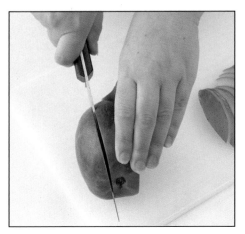

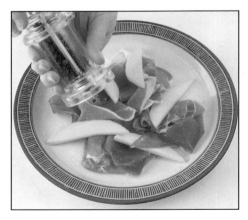

3 Just before serving, arrange the mango slices in among the prosciutto. Grind some black pepper on top and garnish with flat-leaf parsley sprigs.

2 Cut the mango flesh off the pit, then slice and peel it.

CHORIZO IN OLIVE OIL

Spanish chorizo sausage has a deliciously pungent taste; its robust seasoning of garlic, chile and paprika flavors the ingredients it is cooked with. Frying chorizo with onions and olive oil is one of its simplest and most delicious uses.

Preparation time 2 minutes
Cooking time 7–8 minutes

SERVES 4
5 tablespoons extra virgin olive oil
12 ounces chorizo sausage, sliced
1 large onion, thinly sliced
roughly chopped flat-leaf parsley,
  to garnish
warm bread, to serve

1 Heat the oil in a frying pan and sauté the chorizo slices over high heat until they begin to color. Lift out with a slotted spoon.

2 Add the onion to the pan and sauté until colored. Return the sausage slices to the pan and heat through for 1 minute.

3 Pour the mixture into a shallow serving dish and sprinkle with the parsley. Serve with warm bread.

VARIATION
Chorizo is usually available in large supermarkets or delicatessens. Other similarly rich, spicy sausages can be used as a substitute.

GARLIC SHRIMP

For this simple Spanish tapas dish, you really need fresh raw shrimp that will absorb the flavors of the garlic and chile as they fry. Have everything ready for last-minute cooking so that you can take them to the table still sizzling.

Preparation time 5 minutes
Cooking time 5 minutes

SERVES 4
12 ounces – 1 pound large raw shrimp
2 red chiles
5 tablespoons olive oil
3 garlic cloves, crushed
salt and ground black pepper

1 Remove the heads and shells of the shrimp, leaving the tails intact.

2 Halve each chile lengthwise and discard the seeds. Heat the oil in a flameproof pan, suitable for serving. (Alternatively, use a frying pan and have a warmed serving dish ready in the oven.)

3 Add all the shrimp, chiles and garlic to the pan and cook over high heat for about 3 minutes, stirring until the shrimp turn pink. Season lightly with salt and pepper and serve immediately.

MELON, PINEAPPLE AND GRAPE COCKTAIL

A light fresh fruit salad, with no added sugar, makes a refreshing and speedy appetizer.

Preparation time 6 minutes
Cooking time None

SERVES 4

½ melon
8 ounces fresh pineapple
8 ounces seedless green
   grapes, halved
½ cup white grape juice
fresh mint leaves, to garnish

1 Remove the seeds from the melon half and use a melon baller to scoop out even-size balls.

2 Using a sharp knife, cut the skin from the pineapple. Cut the fruit into bite-size chunks.

3 Combine all the fruits in a glass serving dish and pour the white grape juice over them. Serve immediately or cover and chill until required. Garnish with mint leaves.

COOK'S TIP

To save even more time, use an 8-ounce can of pineapple chunks in natural juice. Drain the chunks, reserving the juice in a measuring cup. Make it up to the required quantity for pouring over the fruit with white grape juice.

SMOKED TROUT SALAD

Horseradish is as good a partner to smoked trout as it is to roast beef. In this recipe it is combined with yogurt to make a delicious light salad dressing.

Preparation time 6 minutes
Cooking time None

SERVES 4

1 head oakleaf or other red lettuce
8 ounces small tomatoes, cut into
* thin wedges*
½ cucumber, peeled and thinly sliced
4 smoked trout fillets, about
* 7 ounces each, skinned and flaked*
For the dressing
pinch of mustard powder
3–4 teaspoons white wine vinegar
2 tablespoons light olive oil
scant ½ cup plain yogurt
about 2 tablespoons grated fresh or
* bottled horseradish*
pinch of sugar

1 First, make the dressing. Mix together the mustard powder and vinegar, then gradually whisk in the oil, yogurt, horseradish and sugar.

VARIATION
This salad is equally good with smoked mackerel. Add a garnish of lime or orange slices, slit to the center and twisted.

2 Place the lettuce leaves in a large bowl. Stir the dressing again, then pour half of it over the leaves and toss lightly.

3 Arrange the lettuce on four individual plates with the tomatoes, cucumber and trout. Spoon the remaining dressing over the salads and serve at once.

HOT TOMATO AND MOZZARELLA SALAD

A quick, easy appetizer with a Mediterranean flavor. It can be prepared in advance, chilled, then broiled just before serving.

Preparation time 5 minutes
Cooking time 4–5 minutes

SERVES 4

1 pound plum tomatoes, sliced
8 ounces mozzarella cheese, sliced
1 red onion, finely chopped
4–6 pieces sun-dried tomatoes in oil, drained and chopped
¼ cup olive oil
1 teaspoon red wine vinegar
½ teaspoon Dijon mustard
4 tablespoons chopped fresh mixed herbs, such as basil, parsley, oregano and chives
salt and ground black pepper
fresh herb sprigs, to garnish

1   Arrange the sliced tomatoes and mozzarella in concentric circles in four individual shallow flameproof dishes.

2   Sprinkle the chopped onion and sun-dried tomatoes on top. Preheat the broiler to high.

3   Whisk together the olive oil, vinegar, mustard, chopped herbs and seasoning. Pour over the salads.

4   Place the salads under the hot broiler for 4–5 minutes, until the mozzarella starts to melt. Grind plenty of black pepper over the salads and serve immediately, garnished with fresh herb sprigs, if you like.

ASPARAGUS WITH TARRAGON BUTTER

Eating fresh asparagus with your fingers can be messy, but it is the proper way to eat it!

Preparation time 2 minutes
Cooking time 6–8 minutes

SERVES 4

1¼ pounds fresh asparagus
8 tablespoons (1 stick) butter
2 tablespoons chopped fresh tarragon
1 tablespoon chopped fresh parsley, plus extra to garnish
grated rind of ½ lemon
1 tablespoon lemon juice
salt and ground black pepper

COOK'S TIP

When buying fresh asparagus, choose spears that are plump and have a good, even color with tightly budded tips. The best asparagus is homegrown, because it starts to lose its flavor when cut.

1   Trim the woody ends from the asparagus spears, then tie them into four equal bundles.

2   Place the bundles of asparagus in a large frying pan with about 1 inch boiling water. Cover and cook for about 6–8 minutes, until the asparagus is tender but still firm. Drain well and discard the strings.

3   Meanwhile, melt the butter in a small pan. Add the tarragon, parsley, lemon rind and juice.

4   Arrange the asparagus spears on four warmed serving plates. Season the hot tarragon butter with salt and ground black pepper and pour it over the asparagus. Garnish with more chopped parsley and serve at once.

GUACAMOLE

Tortilla chips are the perfect accompaniment for this classic Mexican dip.

Preparation time 5 minutes
Cooking time None

SERVES 4
2 ripe avocados
2 red chiles, seeded
1 garlic clove
1 shallot
2 tablespoons olive oil, plus extra
to serve
juice of 1 lemon
salt
flat-leaf parsley leaves, to garnish

1 Halve the avocados, remove their pits and, using a spoon, scoop out their flesh into a bowl.

2 Mash the flesh well with a large fork or a potato masher.

3 Finely chop the chiles, garlic and shallot, then stir into the mashed avocado with the olive oil and lemon juice. Add salt to taste.

4 Spoon the mixture into a small serving bowl. Drizzle with a little olive oil and sprinkle a few flat-leaf parsley leaves on top. Serve.

HUMMUS

Serve this nutritious dip with vegetable crudités for a simple and satisfying appetizer, or spread it thickly on hot buttered toast.

Preparation time 5 minutes
Cooking time 2–3 minutes

SERVES 4

14-ounce can chickpeas, drained
2 garlic cloves
*2 tablespoons tahini or unsweetened
smooth peanut butter*
¼ cup olive oil
juice of 1 lemon
½ teaspoon cayenne pepper
1 tablespoon sesame seeds
sea salt

1   Rinse the chickpeas well and place in a blender or food processor with the garlic and a good pinch of sea salt.

2   Add the tahini or peanut butter and process until fairly smooth. With the motor still running, slowly pour in the oil and lemon juice.

COOK'S TIP

Tahini is a thick, smooth and oily paste made from sesame seeds. It is available at health-food stores and large supermarkets. Tahini is a classic ingredient in hummus, this Middle-Eastern dip; peanut butter would not be used in a traditional recipe, but it is a useful substitute.

3   Stir in the cayenne pepper and add more salt to taste. If the mixture is too thick, stir in a little cold water. Transfer the purée to a serving bowl.

4   Heat a small nonstick pan and add the sesame seeds. Cook for 2–3 minutes, shaking the pan, until the seeds are golden. Allow to cool, then sprinkle over the purée.

CHEESE FONDUE

This is a classic fondue in true Swiss style. It should be served with cubes of crusty day-old bread, but it is also good with chunks of spicy cured sausage, such as chorizo.

Preparation time 3 minutes
Cooking time 7 minutes

SERVES 2

1 garlic clove, finely chopped
²/₃ cup dry white wine
5 ounces Gruyère cheese
1 teaspoon cornstarch
1 tablespoon kirsch
salt and ground black pepper
bread or chorizo cubes, to serve

[1] Place the garlic and wine in a small saucepan and bring gently to a boil. Lower the heat and simmer for 3–4 minutes.

COOK'S TIP
Gruyère is a tasty cheese that melts incredibly well. Don't substitute other cheeses in this dish.

[2] Coarsely grate the cheese and stir it into the wine. Continue to stir as the cheese melts.

[3] Blend the cornstarch to a smooth paste with the kirsch and pour it into the pan, stirring. Bring to a boil, stirring constantly until the sauce is smooth and thickened.

[4] Add salt and pepper to taste. Serve immediately in heated bowls or transfer to a fondue pan and keep hot over a chafing dish. Garnish with black pepper and serve with bread or chorizo cubes speared on fondue forks.

CIABATTA WITH MOZZARELLA AND GRILLED ONION

Ciabatta is readily available in most supermarkets. It's even more delicious when made with spinach, sun-dried tomatoes or olives, and you'll probably find these in your local delicatessen.

Preparation time 3 minutes
Cooking time 7 minutes

MAKES 4
1 loaf of ciabatta
¼ cup tomato pesto
2 small mild onions
oil, for brushing
8 ounces mozzarella cheese
8 black olives

1 Preheat the broiler to high. Cut the bread in half horizontally and toast lightly. Spread with the pesto. Leave the broiler on.

VARIATIONS
Toast halved baguettes and top with sliced cherry tomatoes and goat cheese, then broil and garnish with shredded fresh basil.

Toast halved French breads, spread with passata or tomato sauce and top with slices of mozzarella, anchovies and black olives, then broil and garnish with fresh oregano leaves.

2 Peel the onions and cut them horizontally into thick slices. Brush with oil and broil for 3 minutes, until lightly browned.

3 Slice the cheese and arrange over the bread. Lay the onion slices on top and sprinkle on some olives. Place under a hot broiler for 2–3 minutes, until the cheese melts and the onion chars. Cut in half diagonally.

SALAD GREENS WITH GORGONZOLA

Crispy fried pancetta makes a tasty addition and contrasts well in texture and flavor with the softness of mixed salad greens and the sharp taste of Gorgonzola.

Preparation time 5 minutes
Cooking time 5 minutes

SERVES 4

8 ounces pancetta slices, any rinds
  removed, coarsely chopped
2 large garlic cloves, roughly chopped
3 ounces arugula
3 ounces radicchio
½ cup walnuts, roughly chopped
4 ounces Gorgonzola cheese
¼ cup olive oil
1 tablespoon balsamic vinegar
salt and ground black pepper

1 Put the chopped pancetta and garlic in a nonstick or heavy frying pan and heat gently, stirring constantly, until the pancetta renders its fat. Increase the heat and fry until the pancetta and garlic are crisp. Try not to let the garlic brown, or it will acquire a bitter flavor. Remove the pancetta and garlic with a slotted spoon and drain on paper towels. Leave the pancetta drippings in the pan, off the heat.

2 Tear the arugula and radicchio leaves into a salad bowl. Sprinkle with the walnuts, pancetta and garlic. Add salt and pepper and toss to mix. Crumble the Gorgonzola on top.

3 Return the frying pan to medium heat and add the oil and balsamic vinegar to the pancetta drippings. Stir until sizzling, then pour over the salad. Serve at once, to be tossed at the table.

TOMATO AND MOZZARELLA TOASTS

These resemble mini-pizzas and are good with drinks before a dinner party. If you prefer, you can prepare them several hours in advance and pop them in the oven just as your guests arrive.

Preparation time 3 minutes
Cooking time 7 minutes

SERVES 6–8

3 sfilatini (thin ciabatta)
about 1 cup sun-dried tomato paste
3 x 5-ounce packages mozzarella
  cheese, drained and chopped
about 2 teaspoons dried oregano or
  mixed herbs
2–3 tablespoons olive oil
ground black pepper

1 Preheat the oven to 425°F. Also preheat the broiler. Cut each sfilatino on the diagonal into 12–15 slices, discarding the ends. Broil until lightly toasted on both sides. Spread sun-dried tomato paste on one side of each slice of toast. Arrange the mozzarella over the tomato paste.

2 Put the toasts on baking sheets, sprinkle with herbs and pepper to taste and drizzle with oil. Bake for 5 minutes, or until the mozzarella has melted and is bubbling. Let the toasts settle for a few minutes before serving.

CASHEW CHICKEN

In this Chinese-inspired dish, tender pieces of chicken are stir-fried with cashew nuts, red chiles and a touch of garlic.

Preparation time 4 minutes
Cooking time 6 minutes

SERVES 4–6
1 pound boneless chicken breasts
2 tablespoons vegetable oil
2 garlic cloves, sliced
4 dried red chiles, chopped
1 red bell pepper, seeded and diced
2 tablespoons oyster sauce
1 tablespoon soy sauce
1 bunch scallions, cut into
  2-inch lengths
1½ cups cashew nuts, roasted
cilantro leaves, to garnish

1 Remove and discard the skin from the chicken breasts. With a sharp knife, cut the chicken into bite-size pieces and set aside.

2 Heat the oil in a wok and swirl it around. Add the garlic and dried chiles and fry until golden.

3 Add the chicken and stir-fry until it changes color, then add the pepper.

4 Stir in the oyster sauce and soy sauce. Add the scallions and cashew nuts. Stir-fry for 1–2 minutes more. Serve garnished with cilantro leaves.

STIR-FRIED CHICKEN WITH BASIL AND CHILES

This quick and easy chicken dish is an excellent introduction to Thai cuisine. Deep-frying the basil adds another dimension to the dish. Thai basil, which is sometimes known as holy basil, has a unique, pungent flavor that is both spicy and sharp. The dull leaves have serrated edges.

Preparation time 3 minutes
Cooking time 7 minutes

SERVES 4–6
3 tablespoons vegetable oil
4 garlic cloves, sliced
2–4 red chiles, seeded and chopped
1 pound chicken, cut into
  bite-size pieces
2–3 tablespoons fish sauce
2 teaspoons dark soy sauce
1 teaspoon sugar
10–12 Thai basil leaves
2 red chiles, sliced, to garnish
20 Thai basil leaves, deep-fried
  (optional)

1   Heat the oil in a wok or large frying pan and swirl it around.

COOK'S TIP
To deep-fry Thai basil leaves, make sure that the leaves are completely dry. Deep-fry in hot oil for 30–40 seconds, lift out using a slotted spoon and drain on paper towels.

2   Add the garlic and chiles and stir-fry until golden.

3   Add the chicken and stir-fry until it changes color.

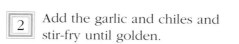

4   Season with fish sauce, soy sauce and sugar. Continue to stir-fry for 3–4 minutes, or until the chicken is cooked. Stir in the fresh Thai basil leaves. Garnish with the chiles and the fried basil, if using.

THAI CHICKEN AND VEGETABLE STIR-FRY

Preparation time 3 minutes
Cooking time 7 minutes

Serves 4
1 lemongrass stalk
½-inch piece of fresh ginger root
1 large garlic clove
2 tablespoons sunflower oil
10 ounces lean chicken, thinly sliced
½ red bell pepper, seeded and sliced
½ green bell pepper, seeded and sliced
4 scallions, chopped
2 carrots, cut into thin sticks
4 ounces haricots verts
2 tablespoons oyster sauce
pinch of sugar
salt and ground black pepper
crushed peanuts and cilantro leaves,
     to garnish

1 Thinly slice the lemongrass. Peel and chop the ginger and garlic. Heat the oil in a frying pan over high heat. Add the lemongrass, ginger and garlic, and stir-fry for 30 seconds, until the garlic is golden and the oil is aromatic.

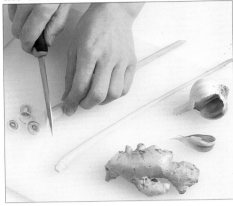

2 Add the chicken and stir-fry for 2 minutes. Then add the vegetables; stir-fry for 3 minutes, until the chicken is cooked and the vegetables are crisp-tender.

3 Finally stir in the oyster sauce, sugar and seasoning to taste and stir-fry for another minute or two to mix and blend well. Serve at once, sprinkled with the peanuts and cilantro leaves. Rice is the traditional accompaniment.

Cook's Tips
Make this quick supper dish a little hotter by adding more fresh ginger root, if you wish. If you can get hold of it, try fresh galangal instead of ginger. The flavor is similar, but has peppery overtones.

CHICKEN WITH TOMATOES AND OLIVES

Chicken breasts or turkey, veal or pork scallops can be flattened for quick and even cooking. You can buy them from the butcher, but they are easy to prepare at home.

Preparation time 5 minutes
Cooking time 5 minutes

SERVES 4

4 skinless boneless chicken breasts
    (5–6 ounces each)
¼ teaspoon cayenne pepper
5–7 tablespoons extra virgin
    olive oil
6 ripe plum tomatoes
1 garlic clove, finely chopped
16–24 pitted black olives
small handful of fresh basil leaves
salt

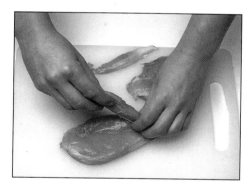

1 Carefully remove the fillets (the long, finger-shaped muscle on the back of each breast) and reserve for another use.

COOK'S TIP

If the tomato skins are at all tough, remove them by cutting a cross in the base of each tomato with a knife, then plunging them into boiling water for about 45 seconds. The skin should simply peel off. If you have a gas stove, you can achieve the same result by preparing the tomatoes in the same way, spearing each one in turn on a fork and rotating it in the open flame until the skin peels back.

2 Place each chicken breast between two sheets of waxed paper or plastic wrap and pound with the flat side of a meat pounder or roll out with a rolling pin to flatten to about ½ inch thick. Season with the cayenne pepper.

3 Heat 3–4 tablespoons of the olive oil in a large, heavy frying pan over medium-high heat. Add the flattened chicken breasts and cook for 3–4 minutes, until golden brown and just cooked, turning them once. Transfer the chicken to warmed serving plates and season with a little salt. Keep the chicken hot.

4 Peel the tomatoes (see Cook's Tip), then seed and chop.

5 Wipe the frying pan and return to the heat. Add another 2–3 tablespoons of olive oil and sauté the garlic for 1 minute, until golden and fragrant. Stir in the olives, cook for another 1 minute, then stir in the tomatoes. Shred the basil leaves and stir into the olive and tomato mixture, then spoon it over the chicken and serve at once.

TURKEY SCALLOPS WITH CAPERS

A staple of bistro cooking, these thin slices of poultry or meat, called scallops or sometimes paillards, cook very quickly and can be served with all kinds of interesting sauces.

Preparation time 6 minutes
Cooking time 4 minutes

SERVES 2

4 thin turkey breast scallops (about 3 ounces each)
1 large unwaxed lemon
½ teaspoon chopped fresh sage
4–5 tablespoons extra virgin olive oil
½ cup fine dry bread crumbs
1 tablespoon capers, rinsed and drained
salt and ground black pepper
sage leaves and lemon wedges, to garnish

1 Place the turkey scallops between two sheets of waxed paper or plastic wrap and pound with the flat side of a meat pounder or roll with a rolling pin to flatten to about a ¼ inch thickness.

2 With a vegetable peeler, remove four pieces of lemon zest. Cut them into thin julienne strips, cover with plastic wrap and set aside. Grate the remainder of the lemon zest and squeeze the lemon. Put the grated zest in a large shallow dish and add the sage, salt and pepper. Stir in 1 tablespoon of the lemon juice, reserving the rest, and about 1 tablespoon of the olive oil, then add the turkey, turn to coat and set aside.

3 Place the bread crumbs in another shallow dish and dip the scallops in the crumbs, coating both sides. In a heavy frying pan, heat 2 tablespoons of the olive oil over high heat, add the scallops and cook for 2–3 minutes, turning once, until golden. Transfer to two warmed plates and keep warm.

4 Wipe the pan, add the remaining oil, the lemon zest julienne and the capers, stirring, and heat through. Spoon a little sauce over the turkey and garnish with sage leaves and lemon.

Veal Scallops with Lemon

Popular in Italian restaurants, this dish is very easy to make at home.

Preparation time 4 minutes
Cooking time 4 minutes

SERVES 4
4 veal scallops
2–3 tablespoons all-purpose flour
¼ cup butter
¼ cup olive oil
¼ cup Italian dry white vermouth or
  dry white wine
3 tablespoons lemon juice
salt and ground black pepper
lemon zest, lemon wedges and fresh
  parsley, to garnish
green beans and peperonata, to serve

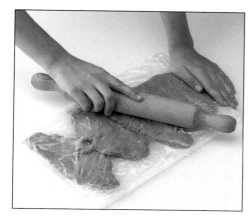

1 Put each scallop between two sheets of waxed paper or plastic wrap and pound until very thin. Cut the pounded scallops in half or quarters and coat in the flour, seasoned with salt and pepper.

Cook's Tip
To make the peperonata suggested as an accompaniment, heat 5 tablespoons olive oil in a pan, add 1 chopped onion, 2 diced red bell peppers, 1 crushed garlic clove and 2 chopped tomatoes and cook gently for 15 minutes. Serve hot or cold.

2 Melt the butter with half the oil in a large, heavy frying pan until sizzling. Add as many scallops as the pan will hold. Cook over medium to high heat for 1–2 minutes on each side, until lightly colored. Remove with a spatula and keep hot. Add the remaining oil and cook the remaining veal scallops in the same way.

3 Remove the pan from the heat and add the vermouth or wine and the lemon juice. Stir vigorously to mix with the pan juices, then return the pan to the heat and return all the veal to the pan. Spoon the sauce over the scallops. Shake the pan over medium heat until all of the scallops are coated in the sauce and heated through.

4 Serve at once, garnished with lemon zest, lemon wedges and parsley. Lightly cooked green beans and peperonata make a delicious accompaniment.

Variation
Use skinless boneless chicken breasts instead of the veal. If they are thick, split them before pounding.

PANFRIED VEAL CHOPS

Veal chops from the loin are an expensive cut and are best cooked quickly and simply. The flavor of basil goes well with veal, but you could use another herb, such as rosemary or parsley.

Preparation time 2 minutes
Cooking time 7–8 minutes

SERVES 2
2 tablespoons butter, softened
1 tablespoon Dijon mustard
1 tablespoon chopped fresh basil
olive oil, for brushing
2 veal loin chops, 1 inch thick (about 8 ounces each)
ground black pepper
fresh basil sprigs, to garnish

1 To make the basil butter, cream the butter with the mustard and chopped basil in a small bowl, then season with pepper.

2 Lightly oil a heavy frying pan or griddle. Set over high heat until very hot but not smoking. Brush both sides of each chop with a little oil and season with a little pepper.

3 Place the chops on the pan or griddle and reduce the heat to medium. Cook for 4–5 minutes, then turn and cook for 3–4 minutes more, until done as preferred (medium-rare meat will still be slightly soft when pressed, medium meat will be springy and well-done firm). Top each chop with half the basil butter and serve, garnished with basil.

VEAL SCALLOPS WITH TARRAGON

These thin slices of veal need little cooking, and the sauce is made very quickly as well.

Preparation time 4 minutes
Cooking time 6 minutes

SERVES 4
4 veal scallops (4–5 ounces each)
1 tablespoon butter
2 tablespoons brandy
1 cup chicken or beef stock
1 tablespoon chopped fresh tarragon
salt and ground black pepper
fresh tarragon sprigs, to garnish

1 Place the veal scallops between two sheets of waxed paper or plastic wrap and pound with the flat side of a meat mallet or roll them with a rolling pin to flatten to about ¼ inch thickness. Season with salt and ground black pepper.

2 Melt the butter in a large frying pan over medium-high heat. Add enough meat to the pan to fit easily in one layer (do not overcrowd the pan; cook in batches if necessary) and cook for 1½–2 minutes, turning once. Each scallop should be lightly browned, but must not be overcooked. Transfer to a platter and cover to keep warm.

3 Add the brandy to the pan, then pour in the stock and bring to a boil. Add the tarragon and continue boiling until the liquid is reduced by half.

4 Return the veal to the pan with any accumulated juices and heat through. Serve immediately, garnished with tarragon sprigs.

CALF'S LIVER WITH HONEY

Liver is the perfect choice for a quick meal. Although it can be braised, it is at its best when cooked briefly in a hot pan. Cook the liver until it is browned on the outside but still rosy pink in the center.

Preparation time 2 minutes
Cooking time 4–5 minutes

SERVES 4

*4 slices calf's liver (about 6 ounces
  each and ½ inch thick)
all-purpose flour, for dusting
2 tablespoons butter
2 tablespoons vegetable oil
2 tablespoons sherry vinegar or red
  wine vinegar
2–3 tablespoons chicken stock
1 tablespoon honey
salt and ground black pepper
watercress sprigs, to garnish*

1   Wipe the liver slices with damp paper towels, then season both sides with a little salt and pepper and dust the slices lightly with flour, shaking off any excess.

COOK'S TIP

It is important to use calf's liver, as it is tender and delicately flavored. You could use lamb's liver, which is difficult to find, but don't use any other type.

2   In a large, heavy frying pan, melt half of the butter with the oil over high heat and swirl to blend thoroughly.

3   Add the liver slices to the pan and cook for 1–2 minutes, until browned on one side, then turn and cook for another 1 minute. Transfer to warmed plates and keep warm.

4   Stir the vinegar, stock and honey into the pan. Boil for about 1 minute, stirring constantly, then add the remaining butter, stirring until melted and smooth. Spoon over the liver slices and garnish with watercress sprigs.

PORK IN SWEET-AND-SOUR SAUCE

The combination of sweet and sour flavors is popular in Venetian cooking, especially with meat and liver. This recipe is given extra bite with the addition of crushed mixed peppercorns. Served with shelled fava beans tossed with grilled bacon, it is delectable.

Preparation time 2–3 minutes
Cooking time 6 minutes

SERVES 2
1 pork tenderloin, about 12 ounces
1½ tablespoons all-purpose flour
2–3 tablespoons olive oil
1 cup dry white wine
2 tablespoons white wine vinegar
2 teaspoons sugar
1 tablespoon mixed peppercorns,
    coarsely ground
salt and ground black pepper
cooked fava beans tossed with bacon,
    to serve

1   Cut the pork diagonally into thin slices. Place between two sheets of plastic wrap and pound lightly with a rolling pin to flatten them.

2   Spread out the flour in a shallow bowl. Season well and coat the meat. Alternatively, put the seasoned flour in a strong plastic bag, add the pork and shake to coat.

3   Heat 1 tablespoon of the oil in a wide, heavy saucepan or frying pan and add as many slices of pork as the pan will hold. Sauté over medium to high heat for 2–3 minutes on each side, until crisp and tender. Remove with a spatula and set aside. Repeat with the remaining pork, adding more oil as necessary.

4   Mix the wine, vinegar and sugar in a measuring cup. Pour into the pan and stir over high heat until reduced. Stir in the peppercorns and return the pork to the pan. Spoon the sauce over the pork until it is evenly coated and heated through. Serve with cooked fava beans tossed with bacon.

PORK WITH CAMEMBERT

When it comes to speedy feasts, pork tenderloin is an excellent choice. Beautifully tender, it needs very little cooking and is delicious served with a creamy cheese sauce.

Preparation time 2 minutes
Cooking time 7–8 minutes

SERVES 3–4
12 ounces–1 pound pork tenderloin
1 tablespoon butter
3 tablespoons sparkling dry cider or dry white wine
½–¾ cup crème fraîche or whipping cream
1 tablespoon chopped fresh mixed herbs, such as marjoram, thyme and sage
½ Camembert cheese (4 ounces), rind removed (2½ ounces without rind), sliced
1½ teaspoons Dijon mustard
ground black pepper
fresh parsley, to garnish

1 Slice the pork tenderloin crosswise into small medallions about ¾ inch thick. Place between two sheets of waxed paper or plastic wrap and pound with the flat side of a meat pounder or roll with a rolling pin to flatten to a thickness of ½ inch. Sprinkle with pepper.

VARIATION
Any creamy cheese that is not too soft can be used instead of Camembert. Try Cambozola or Brie for a change.

2 Melt the butter in a heavy frying pan over medium-high heat until it begins to brown, then add the meat. Cook, turning once, for 5 minutes, or until just cooked through and the meat is springy when pressed. Transfer to a warmed dish and cover to keep warm.

3 Add the cider or wine and bring to a boil, scraping the bottom of the pan. Stir in the cream and herbs and bring back to a boil.

4 Add the cheese and mustard and any accumulated juices from the meat. Stir until the cheese melts. Add a little more cream if needed and adjust the seasoning. Serve the pork with the sauce and garnish with parsley.

SALMON WITH GREEN PEPPERCORNS

A fashionable discovery of nouvelle cuisine, green peppercorns add piquancy to all kinds of sauces and stews. Available pickled in jars or cans, they are great to keep on hand in your pantry.

Preparation time 1 minute
Cooking time 9 minutes

SERVES 4

1 tablespoon butter
2 or 3 shallots, finely chopped
1 tablespoon brandy (optional)
¼ cup dry white wine
6 tablespoons fish or chicken stock
½ cup whipping cream
2–3 tablespoons green peppercorns in brine, rinsed and drained
1–2 tablespoons vegetable oil
4 pieces salmon fillet (6–7 ounces each)
salt and ground black pepper
fresh parsley, to garnish

1 Melt the butter in a heavy saucepan over medium heat. Add the shallots and cook for 1 minute, until just softened.

2 Add the brandy, if using, and the white wine. Stir well, then pour in the stock and bring to a boil. Continue to boil rapidly until the liquid has reduced by three-quarters, stirring occasionally.

3 Reduce the heat, then add the cream and half the green peppercorns, crushing them slightly with the back of a spoon. Cook very gently for 4 minutes, until the sauce is slightly thickened, then strain and stir in the remaining peppercorns. Keep the sauce warm over very low heat, stirring occasionally, while you cook the salmon.

4 In a large, heavy frying pan, heat the oil over medium-high heat until very hot. Lightly season the salmon and cook for 3–4 minutes, or until the flesh is opaque and flakes easily when tested with the tip of a sharp knife. Arrange the fish on warmed plates and pour the sauce over it. Garnish with parsley.

HALIBUT WITH TOMATO VINAIGRETTE

Sauce vièrge, a lightly cooked mixture of tomatoes, aromatic fresh herbs and olive oil, can either be served at room temperature or, as in this dish, slightly warm.

Preparation time 4 minutes
Cooking time 5–6 minutes

SERVES 2

3 large ripe beefsteak tomatoes, peeled, seeded and chopped
2 shallots or 1 small red onion, finely chopped
1 garlic clove, crushed
6 tablespoons chopped mixed fresh herbs, such as parsley, cilantro, basil, tarragon, chervil or chives
½ cup extra virgin olive oil, plus extra for greasing
4 halibut fillets or steaks (6–7 ounces each)
salt and ground black pepper
green salad, to serve

1 In a saucepan, mix together the tomatoes, shallots or onion, garlic and herbs. Stir in the oil and season with salt and ground black pepper. Cover the pan and let the sauce stand at room temperature while you broil the fish.

COOK'S TIP
If time permits, set aside the sauce for up to an hour.

2 Preheat the broiler. Line a pan with foil and brush the foil lightly with oil.

3 Season the fish with salt and pepper. Place the fish on the foil and brush with a little extra oil. Broil for 5–6 minutes, until the flesh is opaque and the top lightly browned.

4 Meanwhile, heat the sauce gently for a few minutes. Serve the fish with the sauce and a salad.

Panfried Sole with Lemon Butter Sauce

The delicate flavor and texture of sole is brought out in this simple, classic recipe. Lemon sole is used here because it is easier to obtain—and much less expensive—than Dover sole.

Preparation time 1 minute
Cooking time 9 minutes

Serves 2
2–3 tablespoons all-purpose flour
4 lemon sole fillets
3 tablespoons olive oil
4 tablespoons butter
¼ cup lemon juice
2 tablespoons rinsed capers
salt and ground black pepper
fresh flat-leaf parsley and lemon
  wedges, to garnish

1   Season the flour with salt and black pepper. Coat the sole fillets evenly on both sides. Heat the oil with half the butter in a large shallow pan until foaming. Add two sole fillets and sauté over medium heat for 2–3 minutes on each side.

2   Lift out the sole fillets with a spatula and place on a warmed serving platter. Keep hot. Sauté the remaining sole fillets in the same way, then lift them out carefully and add them to the platter.

3   Remove the pan from the heat and add the lemon juice and remaining butter. Return the pan to high heat and stir vigorously until the pan juices are sizzling and beginning to turn golden brown. Remove from the heat and stir in the capers.

4   Pour the pan juices over the sole, sprinkle with salt and pepper to taste and garnish with the parsley. Add the lemon wedges and serve at once.

Cook's Tips

It is important to cook the pan juices to the right color after removing the fish. Too pale, and they will taste insipid, too dark, and they may taste bitter. Take great care not to be distracted at this point so that you can watch the color of the juices change to a golden brown. If you don't like the flavor of capers, leave them out. The butter sauce is good enough to serve on its own.

SHRIMP AND VEGETABLE BALTI

A delicious accompaniment to other dishes from the Balti region of Pakistan. Double the quantities if serving it solo.

Preparation time 3 minutes
Cooking time 7 minutes

SERVES 4
6 ounces cooked, peeled shrimp
2 tablespoons corn oil
¼ teaspoon nigella (black onion seeds)
4–6 curry leaves
1 cup frozen peas
⅔ cup frozen corn
1 large zucchini, sliced
1 red bell pepper, seeded and
  roughly diced
1 teaspoon crushed coriander seeds
1 teaspoon crushed dried red chiles
1 tablespoon lemon juice
salt
1 tablespoon cilantro leaves, to
  garnish

1 Drain any excess liquid from the shrimp and pat them dry on paper towels. Heat the oil with the nigella and curry leaves in a nonstick wok or frying pan.

COOK'S TIP
The best way to crush whole seeds is to use an electric spice grinder or a small marble mortar and pestle.

2 Add the shrimp to the wok or frying pan and stir-fry until any liquid has evaporated.

3 Add the peas, corn, zucchini and pepper and stir-fry for 3–5 minutes more.

4 Add the coriander seeds, dried chiles and lemon juice. Toss over the heat for 1 minute, season to taste and serve, garnished with the cilantro leaves.

GREEN SHRIMP CURRY

A popular, fragrant, creamy curry that takes very little time to prepare. It can also be made with thin strips of chicken.

Preparation time 2 minutes
Cooking time 8 minutes

SERVES 4–6
2 tablespoons vegetable oil
2 tablespoons green curry paste
1 pound raw large shrimp, shelled
    and deveined
4 kaffir lime leaves, torn
1 lemongrass stalk, bruised
    and chopped
1 cup coconut milk
2 tablespoons fish sauce
½ cucumber, seeded and cut into
    thin sticks
10–15 basil leaves
sliced green chiles, to garnish

1   Heat the oil in a frying pan. Add the green curry paste and sauté until bubbling and fragrant.

2   Add the shrimp, lime leaves and lemongrass. Sauté for about 2 minutes, until the shrimp are pink.

3   Stir in the coconut milk and bring to a gentle boil. Simmer, stirring, for about 5 minutes, or until the shrimp are tender.

4   Stir in the fish sauce and cucumber. Tear the basil leaves and add them too, then top with the chiles and serve.

SAUTEED SCALLOPS

Scallops go well with all sorts of sauces, but simple cooking is the best way to enjoy their delicate, fresh-from-the-sea flavor.

Preparation time 1 minute
Cooking time 5 minutes

SERVES 2
1 pound sea scallops
2 tablespoons butter
2 tablespoons dry white vermouth
1 tablespoon finely chopped
* fresh parsley*
salt and ground black pepper

1 Rinse the scallops under cold running water to remove any sand or grit. Drain them well and pat dry using paper towels. Spread them out and season them lightly with salt and pepper.

2 In a frying pan large enough to hold the scallops in one layer, heat half the butter until it begins to color. Sauté the scallops for 3–5 minutes, turning, until golden brown on both sides and just firm to the touch. Remove to a serving platter and cover to keep hot.

3 Add the vermouth to the hot frying pan, swirl in the remaining butter, stir in the parsley and pour the sauce over the scallops. Serve immediately.

GARLICKY SCALLOPS AND SHRIMP

Scallops and shrimp provide a healthy meal in next to no time. This method of cooking comes from France and is popular in Provence.

Preparation time 1 minute
Cooking time 4–5 minutes

SERVES 2–4
6 large sea scallops
6–8 large raw shrimp, peeled, tails
* left intact*
all-purpose flour, for dusting
2–3 tablespoons olive oil
1 garlic clove, finely chopped
1 tablespoon chopped fresh basil
2–3 tablespoons lemon juice
salt and ground black pepper

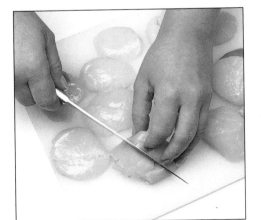

1 Rinse the scallops under cold running water to remove any sand or grit. Drain, then pat dry using paper towels. Cut them in half crosswise. Season the scallops and shrimp with salt and pepper and dust lightly with flour. Heat the oil in a large frying pan over high heat and add the scallops and shrimp.

2 Reduce the heat slightly and cook for 2 minutes, then turn the scallops and shrimp and add the garlic and basil, shaking the pan to distribute them evenly. Cook for another 2 minutes, until the scallops are golden and just firm to the touch. Sprinkle with the lemon juice and toss to blend. Serve at once.

NOODLES WITH PINEAPPLE, GINGER AND CHILES

Preparation and
cooking time 8–10 minutes

Serves 4
10 ounces dried noodles
4 fresh or drained, canned
  pineapple rings
3 tablespoons light brown sugar
¼ cup fresh lime juice
¼ cup coconut milk
2 tablespoons fish sauce
2 tablespoons grated fresh ginger root
2 garlic cloves, finely chopped
1 ripe mango or 2 peaches,
  finely diced
For the garnish
2 shallots, sliced
2 red chiles, shredded
fresh mint leaves

1. Cook the noodles in a large saucepan of boiling water until tender, following the directions on the package.

2. Meanwhile, place the pineapple rings in a flameproof dish, sprinkle with 2 tablespoons of the sugar and broil until golden. Cut into small dice.

3. Mix the lime juice, coconut milk and fish sauce in a salad bowl. Add the remaining brown sugar with the ginger and garlic and whisk well. Drain the noodles, refresh under cold water and drain again. Add to the bowl with the noodles and pineapple.

4. Add the mango or peaches and toss lightly. Sprinkle the scallions, chiles and mint on top. Serve.

BUCKWHEAT NOODLES WITH SMOKED SALMON

Young pea shoots are only available for a short time. You can substitute watercress, young leeks or your favorite green vegetable or herb in this dish.

Preparation and
cooking time 8–10 minutes

Serves 4
8 ounces buckwheat or soba noodles
1 tablespoon oyster sauce
juice of ½ lemon
2–3 tablespoons light olive oil
4 ounces smoked salmon, cut into
  fine strips
4 ounces young pea shoots
2 ripe tomatoes, peeled, seeded and
  cut into strips
1 tablespoon snipped chives
salt and ground black pepper

1. Cook the buckwheat or soba noodles in a large saucepan of boiling water, following the directions on the package. Drain, then pour into a colander and rinse under cold running water. Drain well, shaking the colander to extract any remaining water.

2. Pour the noodles into a large bowl. Add the oyster sauce and lemon juice and season with pepper to taste. Moisten with the olive oil.

3. Add the smoked salmon, pea shoots, tomatoes and chives. Mix well and serve at once.

TAGLIATELLE WITH PROSCIUTTO AND ASPARAGUS

This stunning dish is very easy to make. Serve it for a special occasion.

Preparation and
cooking time 7–10 minutes

SERVES 4

12 ounces fresh or dried tagliatelle
2 tablespoons butter
1 tablespoon olive oil
8 ounces asparagus tips
1 garlic clove, chopped
4 ounces prosciutto, sliced into strips
2 tablespoons chopped fresh sage
²/₃ cup light cream
4 ounces Double Gloucester cheese or
    aged cheddar cheese, grated
4 ounces Gruyère cheese, grated
fresh sage leaves, to garnish

1 Cook the pasta in a large saucepan of boiling water until tender, following the instructions on the package.

2 Meanwhile, melt the butter and oil in a frying pan and gently sauté the asparagus tips for 3–4 minutes, or until almost tender.

3 Stir in the garlic and prosciutto and cook for 1 minute.

4 Stir in the sage leaves and cook for 1 minute more, then pour in the cream. Bring to a boil over medium heat, stirring frequently.

5 Add the grated Double Gloucester or aged cheddar and Gruyère cheeses. Simmer gently, stirring occasionally, until thoroughly melted. Season to taste. Drain the pasta well and pour it into a bowl. Add the sauce and toss to coat. Serve immediately, garnished with fresh sage.

RAVIOLI WITH FOUR-CHEESE SAUCE

This smooth cheesy sauce coats the pasta evenly.

Preparation and
cooking time 5–6 minutes

SERVES 4

12 ounces fresh ravioli
4 tablespoons butter
½ cup all-purpose flour
scant 2 cups milk
2 ounces Parmesan cheese
2 ounces Edam cheese
2 ounces Gruyère cheese
2 ounces Fontina cheese
salt and ground black pepper
chopped fresh flat-leaf parsley,
   to garnish

| 1 | Cook the pasta following the instructions on the package. |

| 2 | Meanwhile, melt the butter in a saucepan, stir in the flour and cook for 2 minutes, stirring. |

| 3 | Gradually stir in the milk until well blended. |

| 4 | Bring the milk to a boil over low heat, stirring constantly until thickened. |

| 5 | Grate the cheeses and stir them into the sauce. Stir until they are just beginning to melt. Remove the sauce from the heat and season with salt and pepper. |

| 6 | Drain the pasta thoroughly and turn it into a large serving bowl. Pour on the sauce and toss to coat. Serve immediately, garnished with the chopped fresh parsley. |

COOK'S TIP

If you cannot find all of the above cheeses, simply substitute your favorites. The aim is to have a total quantity of 8 ounces of cheese and to include Parmesan in the selection. Always buy Parmesan in the piece and grate it yourself—using already-grated cheese may save time, but the flavor will not be as good.

SPAGHETTI ALLA CARBONARA

This is a classic pasta dish. If you use fresh spaghetti, cook it at the last minute, as it takes very little time.

Preparation and
cooking time 7–10 minutes

SERVES 4

12 ounces spaghetti
1 tablespoon olive oil
1 onion, chopped
4 ounces bacon or pancetta, diced
1 garlic clove, chopped
3 eggs
1¼ cups heavy cream
2 ounces Parmesan cheese (½ cup when grated)
salt and ground black pepper
chopped fresh basil, to garnish

1 Cook the pasta following the instructions on the package.

2 Meanwhile, heat the oil in a frying pan and sauté the onion and bacon for 5 minutes, until softened. Stir in the garlic and sauté for 2 minutes more, stirring.

3 Meanwhile, beat the eggs in a bowl, then stir in the cream and season with salt and pepper. Grate the Parmesan cheese and stir it into the cream mixture.

4 Stir the cream mixture into the onion and bacon and cook over low heat for a few minutes, stirring constantly until heated through. Season to taste.

5 Drain the pasta thoroughly and turn it into a large serving bowl. Pour on the sauce and toss to coat. Serve immediately, garnished with chopped fresh basil.

COOK'S TIPS

Italians would use pancetta, which is lightly cured but similar to bacon. You can buy it in most supermarkets and delicatessens. If you use bacon, you can parboil it to lessen the smoky flavor.

SPINACH TAGLIARINI WITH ASPARAGUS

Fresh pasta is a boon to the busy cook. You may not be able to locate spinach tagliarini, but any fresh pasta will work just as well.

Preparation time 2–4 minutes
Cooking time 6–8 minutes

SERVES 4–6

2 skinless, boneless chicken breasts
1 tablespoon light soy sauce
2 tablespoons sherry
2 tablespoons cornstarch
8 shallots, cut into 1-inch diagonal
  slices
1–2 garlic cloves, crushed
zest of ½ lemon, in fine julienne strips
⅔ cup chicken stock
1 teaspoon sugar
2 tablespoons lemon juice
8 ounces slender asparagus spears,
  cut into 3-inch lengths
1 pound fresh spinach tagliarini or
  other fresh pasta
salt and ground black pepper

[1] Place the chicken breasts between two sheets of plastic wrap and flatten to a thickness of ¼ inch with a rolling pin. Using a sharp knife, cut the chicken across the grain into 1-inch strips. Put the chicken into a bowl with the soy sauce, sherry, cornstarch and seasoning. Toss to coat each piece.

COOK'S TIP
Fresh pasta is ready as soon as it rises to the surface of the boiling water.

[2] Put the chicken, shallots, garlic and lemon zest in a large nonstick frying pan. Add the stock and bring to a boil, stirring constantly until thickened. Add the sugar, lemon juice and asparagus. Simmer for 4–5 minutes, until tender.

[3] Meanwhile, cook the pasta in a large pan of boiling salted water for 2–3 minutes, until just tender. Drain thoroughly. Arrange on serving plates and spoon the chicken and asparagus sauce over it. Serve the dish immediately.

FRENCH GOAT CHEESE SALAD

Preparation time 2–3 minutes
Cooking time 6 minutes

SERVES 4
7 ounces prepared mixed
  salad greens
4 strips bacon
4 ounces full-fat goat cheese
16 thin slices French bread
For the dressing
¼ cup olive oil
1 tablespoon tarragon vinegar
2 teaspoons walnut oil
1 teaspoon Dijon mustard
1 teaspoon whole-grain mustard
salt and ground black pepper

1 Preheat the broiler to medium heat. Rinse and dry the salad greens, then arrange in four individual bowls. Place the ingredients for the dressing in a screw-top jar, shake well and reserve.

2 Lay the bacon on a board, then stretch with the back of a knife and cut each into four pieces. Roll each piece up and broil for 2–3 minutes.

3 Meanwhile, slice the goat cheese into eight pieces and halve each slice. Top each slice of bread with a piece of goat cheese and place under the broiler. Turn the bacon and continue cooking with the goat cheese toasts until the cheese is golden and bubbling.

4 Arrange the bacon rolls and toasts on top of the prepared salad greens. Shake the dressing well and pour a little over each salad. Serve at once.

VARIATION
If you prefer, just slice the goat cheese and place on toasted French bread. Or use whole-wheat toast for a nutty flavor.

GREEK SALAD PITAS

Horiatiki is the Greek name for this classic salad made with feta—a sheep's milk cheese. It is great in hot pita breads.

Preparation time 5 minutes
Cooking time 2 minutes

MAKES 4
1 cup diced feta cheese
¼ cucumber, peeled and diced
8 cherry tomatoes, quartered
½ small green bell pepper, seeded and
  thinly sliced
¼ small onion, thinly sliced
8 black olives, pitted and halved
2 tablespoons olive oil
1 teaspoon dried oregano
4 large pita breads
¼ cup plain yogurt
1 teaspoon dried mint
salt and ground black pepper
fresh mint, to garnish

1 Place the cheese, cucumber, tomatoes, pepper, onion and olives in a bowl. Stir in the olive oil and oregano, then season well and set the bowl aside.

2 Place the pita breads in a toaster or under a preheated broiler for about 2 minutes, until puffed up. Meanwhile, to make the dressing, mix the yogurt with the mint, season well and set aside.

3 Holding the hot pitas in a kitchen towel, slice each one from top to bottom down one of the longer sides and open out to form a pocket.

4 Divide the prepared salad among the pita bread pockets and drizzle with a spoonful of the yogurt dressing. Serve the filled pitas immediately, garnished with fresh mint. Offer the remaining dressing separately.

Spinach Salad with Bacon and Shrimp

Preparation time 4 minutes
Cooking time 6 minutes

SERVES 4

7 tablespoons olive oil
2 tablespoons sherry vinegar
2 garlic cloves, finely chopped
1 teaspoon Dijon mustard
12 cooked large shrimp
4 ounces bacon, cut into strips
about 4 ounces fresh young
* spinach leaves*
½ head oakleaf lettuce, roughly torn
salt and ground black pepper

1 To make the dressing, whisk together 6 tablespoons of the olive oil with the vinegar, garlic, mustard and seasoning in a small pan. Heat gently until thickened slightly, then keep warm.

2 Carefully peel the shrimp, leaving the tails intact.

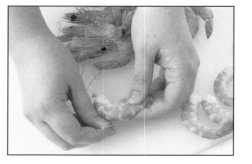

3 Heat the remaining oil in a frying pan and fry the bacon until golden and crisp, stirring occasionally. Add the shrimp and stir-fry until warmed through.

4 Trim the spinach leaves and arrange them with the torn oakleaf lettuce on four individual serving plates.

5 Spoon the bacon and shrimp onto the greens, then pour on the hot dressing. Serve at once.

COOK'S TIP
Sherry vinegar lends its pungent flavor to this delicious salad. You can buy it at large supermarkets and good delicatessens.

CAESAR SALAD

For this famous salad, created in the 1920s by the Tijuana chef called Caesar Cardini, the dressing is traditionally tossed into crunchy romaine lettuce, but any crisp lettuce will do.

Preparation time 2 minutes
Cooking time 6–8 minutes

SERVES 4
1 large head romaine lettuce
4 thick slices white or whole-wheat
  bread without crusts, cubed
3 tablespoons olive oil
1 garlic clove, crushed
¼ cup grated Parmesan cheese
For the dressing
1 egg
1 garlic clove, chopped
2 tablespoons lemon juice
dash of Worcestershire sauce
3 anchovy fillets, chopped
½ cup olive oil
salt and ground black pepper

1 Preheat the oven to 425°F. Separate, rinse and dry the lettuce leaves. Tear the outer leaves roughly and chop the heart roughly.

2 Arrange the lettuce in a salad bowl. Mix together the cubed bread, olive oil and garlic in a separate bowl. Let sit for 2 minutes, until the bread has soaked up the flavored oil. Lay the bread cubes on a baking sheet and place in the oven for 6–8 minutes (keeping an eye on them), until golden brown.

3 Meanwhile, make the dressing. Break the egg in a food processor or blender and add the garlic, lemon juice, Worcestershire sauce and one of the anchovy fillets.

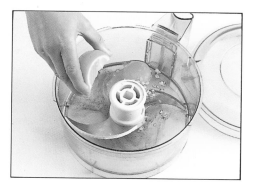

4 Blend the mixture until smooth. With the motor running, pour in the olive oil in a thin stream until the dressing has the consistency of light cream.

5 Season the dressing with ground black pepper and a little salt if needed. Pour it over the lettuce and toss well, then toss with the garlic croutons, Parmesan cheese and the remaining anchovies and serve.

WARM CHICKEN LIVER SALAD

This popular salad makes an excellent light lunch. For a more substantial dish, cook three or four slices of bacon and crumble them over the salad.

Preparation time 4–5 minutes
Cooking time 4–5 minutes

SERVES 4
4 ounces each young spinach leaves, arugula and lollo rossa lettuce
2 pink grapefruit
6 tablespoons sunflower oil
2 teaspoons dark sesame oil
2 teaspoons soy sauce
8 ounces chicken livers, chopped
salt and ground black pepper

1 Wash, dry and tear up all the spinach and salad greens. Mix them together well in a large salad bowl. Cut away the peel and white pith from the grapefruit, then segment them, catching the juice in a bowl. Add the segments to the greens in the bowl.

2 Mix 4 tablespoons sunflower oil with sesame oil, soy sauce and grapefruit juice to taste.

3 Heat the rest of the sunflower oil in a small pan and cook the livers for 4–5 minutes, until firm and lightly browned, stirring occasionally.

4 Place the chicken livers on the salad greens. Season the dressing with salt and pepper, drizzle it over the salad and serve at once.

THAI-STYLE CABBAGE SALAD

A simple and delicious way of using cabbage. Broccoli and cauliflower can also be prepared this way.

Preparation time 6 minutes
Cooking time 4 minutes

SERVES 4–6
2 tablespoons fish sauce
grated zest of 1 lime
2 tablespoons lime juice
½ cup coconut milk
2 tablespoons vegetable oil
2 large red chiles, seeded and finely
   cut into strips
6 garlic cloves, finely sliced
6 shallots, finely sliced
1 small cabbage, shredded
2 tablespoons coarsely chopped
   roasted peanuts, to serve (optional)

1   Make the dressing. Whisk the fish sauce with the lime zest and juice and coconut milk.

2   Heat the oil in a wok or frying pan. Stir-fry the chiles, garlic and shallots until the shallots are brown and crisp.

3   Bring a saucepan of lightly salted water to a boil. Add the cabbage and blanch for about 2 minutes. Drain thoroughly, then place the cabbage in a bowl.

4   Stir the dressing into the cabbage, toss and mix well. Transfer the salad to a serving dish. Sprinkle with the fried shallot mixture and the coarsely chopped roasted peanuts, if using.

CHICORY SALAD WITH BACON

Young dandelion leaves can replace the chicory or escarole leaves and the salad can be sprinkled with chopped hard-boiled egg.

Preparation time 3–4 minutes
Cooking time 6 minutes

SERVES 4

8 ounces chicory or escarole leaves
5–6 tablespoons extra virgin
  olive oil
6-ounce piece of bacon, diced, or 6
  slices thick-cut bacon, cut crosswise
  into thin strips
1 cup white bread cubes
1 small garlic clove, finely chopped
1 tablespoon red wine vinegar
2 teaspoons Dijon mustard
salt and ground black pepper

1   Tear the chicory or escarole into bite-size pieces and put them in a salad bowl.

COOK'S TIP

Use chicory or escarole leaves as soon as possible after purchase. To store, wrap the leaves in a plastic bag and place in the vegetable bin of the refrigerator for up to three days.

2   Heat 1 tablespoon of the oil in a frying pan and add the bacon. Fry until crisp and browned, then remove with a slotted spoon and drain on paper towels.

3   Add 2 tablespoons of oil to the pan and fry the bread cubes over medium-high heat, turning frequently, until evenly browned. Remove with a slotted spoon and drain on paper towels.

4   Put the garlic, vinegar and mustard into the pan with the remaining oil and heat until just warm, whisking. Season to taste, then pour over the salad and sprinkle with the fried bacon and croutons.

Green Bean and Sweet Red Pepper Salad

Preparation time 5–6 minutes
Cooking time None

Serves 4

12 ounces cooked green beans,
  quartered
2 red bell peppers, seeded and chopped
2 shallots, chopped
1 or more drained pickled serrano
  chiles, well rinsed and then seeded
  and chopped
1 head iceberg lettuce, coarsely
  shredded, or mixed salad greens
olives, to garnish

For the dressing

3 tablespoons red wine vinegar
9 tablespoons olive oil
salt and ground black pepper

1 Combine the green beans, peppers, shallots and chiles in a salad bowl.

2 Make the dressing. Pour the red wine vinegar into a bowl or cup. Add salt and ground black pepper to taste, then whisk in the olive oil until well combined.

3 Pour half the salad dressing over the prepared vegetables and toss lightly together to mix and coat thoroughly. Taste the mixture and add more dressing if required, or offer it separately.

4 Line a large platter with the shredded lettuce leaves and arrange the dressed vegetable mixture attractively on top. Garnish with the olives and serve, with any extra dressing.

WARM FAVA BEAN AND FETA SALAD

This recipe is loosely based on a typical medley of fresh-tasting Greek salad ingredients—fava beans, tomatoes and feta cheese. It's lovely warm or cold as a first course or main course accompaniment.

Preparation time 2 minutes
Cooking time 4–5 minutes

SERVES 4–6

2 pounds fava beans, shelled
¼ cup olive oil
6 ounces plum tomatoes, halved, or quartered if large
4 garlic cloves, crushed
4 ounces firm feta cheese, cut into chunks
3 tablespoons chopped fresh dill, plus extra to garnish
12 black olives
salt and ground black pepper

1 Cook the fava beans in boiling, salted water until just tender. Drain and set aside.

3 Add the feta to the pan and toss the ingredients together for 1 minute. Place in a salad bowl and mix with the drained beans, dill, olives and salt and pepper. Serve garnished with chopped dill.

2 Meanwhile, heat the oil in a heavy frying pan and add the tomatoes and garlic. Cook over high heat until the tomatoes are beginning to color.

HALOUMI AND GRAPE SALAD

Haloumi, a Greek cheese, is delicious fried. Its salty flavor is the ideal foil for grapes and salad greens.

Preparation time 2 minutes
Cooking time 2–3 minutes

SERVES 4

5 ounces mixed salad greens
¾ cup each seedless green and red grapes
9 ounces haloumi cheese
3 tablespoons olive oil
fresh young thyme leaves and basil sprigs, to garnish
For the dressing
¼ cup olive oil
1 tablespoon lemon juice
½ teaspoon sugar
salt and ground black pepper
1 tablespoon chopped fresh thyme or dill

1 To make the dressing, whisk together the olive oil, lemon juice and sugar. Season with salt and pepper. Stir in the thyme or dill and set aside.

2 Toss together the salad greens and the green and red grapes, then transfer to a large serving plate.

3 Thinly slice the cheese. Heat the oil in a large frying pan. Add the cheese and fry briefly until it turns golden on the underside. Turn the cheese with a spatula and cook the other side.

4 Arrange the cheese over the salad. Pour on the dressing and garnish with thyme and basil.

TURKISH SALAD

This classic salad is a wonderful combination of textures and flavors. The saltiness of the cheese is perfectly balanced by the refreshing salad vegetables.

Preparation time 8–10 minutes
Cooking time None

SERVES 4
1 romaine lettuce heart
1 green bell pepper
1 red bell pepper
½ cucumber
4 tomatoes
1 red onion
8 ounces feta cheese, crumbled
black olives, to garnish
For the dressing
3 tablespoons olive oil
3 tablespoons lemon juice
1 garlic clove, crushed
1 tablespoon chopped fresh parsley
1 tablespoon chopped fresh mint
salt and ground black pepper

1 Chop the lettuce into bite-size pieces. Seed the peppers, remove the cores and cut the flesh into thin strips. Chop the cucumber and slice or chop the tomatoes. Cut the onion in half, then slice finely.

2 Place the chopped lettuce, peppers, cucumber, tomatoes and onion in a large bowl. Sprinkle the feta over the top and toss lightly.

3 Make the dressing. Whisk together the olive oil, lemon juice and garlic in a small bowl. Stir in the chopped fresh parsley and mint and season with salt and ground black pepper to taste.

4 Pour the dressing over the salad, toss lightly and serve at once, garnished with a handful of black olives.

PERSIAN SALAD

Some of the simplest dishes are also the most successful. This salad is made in minutes and has a crisp, fresh flavor. Serve it with cold meats and baked potatoes.

Preparation time 5 minutes
Cooking time None

SERVES 2
4 tomatoes
½ cucumber
1 onion
1 romaine lettuce heart
For the dressing
2 tablespoons olive oil
juice of 1 lemon
1 garlic clove, crushed
salt and ground black pepper

1 Cut the tomatoes and cucumber into small cubes. Finely chop the onion and tear the lettuce into bite-size pieces.

2 Place the tomatoes, cucumber, onion and lettuce in a large salad bowl and mix lightly together.

3 To make the dressing, pour the olive oil into a small bowl. Add the lemon juice and garlic and whisk together well. Stir in salt to taste. Pour over the salad and toss lightly to mix. Sprinkle with black pepper and serve at once.

SHRIMP NOODLE SALAD WITH FRAGRANT HERBS

A light, refreshing salad with all the tangy flavor of the sea. Instead of shrimp, try squid, scallops, mussels or crab.

Preparation time 8 minutes
Cooking time 1 minute

SERVES 4

4 ounces cellophane noodles, soaked
  in hot water until soft
16 cooked shrimp, peeled
1 small green bell pepper, seeded and
  cut into strips
½ cucumber, cut into strips
1 tomato, cut into strips
2 shallots, finely sliced
salt and ground black pepper
cilantro leaves, to garnish

For the dressing
1 tablespoon rice vinegar
2 tablespoons fish sauce
2 tablespoons fresh lime juice
pinch of salt
½ teaspoon grated fresh ginger root
1 lemongrass stalk, finely chopped
1 red chile, seeded and sliced
2 tablespoons roughly chopped mint
few sprigs tarragon, roughly chopped
1 tablespoon snipped chives

1   Make the dressing by mixing all the ingredients in a small bowl or cup; whisk well.

3   In a large bowl, combine the noodles with the shrimp, pepper, cucumber, tomato and shallots. Lightly season with salt and pepper, then toss with the dressing.

2   Drain the noodles, then plunge them into a saucepan of boiling water for 1 minute. Drain, rinse under cold running water and drain again.

4   Spoon the noodle mixture onto individual plates, arranging the shrimp on top. Garnish with a few cilantro leaves and serve at once.

COOK'S TIPS
Shrimp are available cooked and peeled. To cook raw shrimp, boil them for 5 minutes, or until they turn pink. Let them cool in the cooking liquid, then gently pull off the tail shell and twist off the head.

THAI NOODLE SALAD

The addition of coconut milk and sesame oil gives an unusual nutty flavor to the dressing for this colorful noodle salad.

Preparation time 5 minutes
Cooking time 5 minutes

SERVES 4–6

12 ounces somen noodles
1 large carrot, cut into thin strips
1 bunch asparagus, trimmed and cut into 1½-inch lengths
1 red bell pepper, seeded and cut into fine strips
4 ounces snow peas, trimmed and halved
4 ounces baby corn, halved lengthwise
4 ounces bean sprouts
4-ounce can water chestnuts, drained and finely sliced

For the dressing

3 tablespoons roughly torn basil
5 tablespoons roughly chopped mint
1 cup coconut milk
2 tablespoons dark sesame oil
1 tablespoon grated fresh ginger root
2 garlic cloves, finely chopped
juice of 1 lime
2 shallots, finely chopped
salt and cayenne pepper

To garnish

1 lime, cut into wedges
½ cup roasted peanuts, roughly chopped
cilantro leaves

VARIATIONS
Use shredded omelet or sliced hard-boiled eggs to garnish the salad.

1. Make the dressing. Combine the basil, mint, coconut milk, sesame oil, ginger, garlic, lime juice and shallots in a bowl and mix well. Season to taste with salt and cayenne pepper.

2. Cook the noodles in a large saucepan of boiling water until just tender, following the directions on the package.

3. Meanwhile, cook the vegetables in separate pans of boiling salted water until crisp-tender. Drain, plunge them into cold water and drain again. Drain and refresh the noodles in the same way.

4. Toss the noodles, vegetables and dressing together. Arrange on serving plates and garnish with the lime, peanuts and cilantro.

CABBAGE SLAW WITH DATES AND APPLES

Three types of cabbage are shredded together for serving raw, so that the maximum amount of vitamin C is retained in this cheerful and speedy salad. It makes a very good light lunch.

Preparation time 8 minutes
Cooking time None

SERVES 6–8

¼ small white cabbage, shredded
¼ small red cabbage, shredded
¼ small Savoy cabbage, shredded
1 cup dried pitted dates
3 eating apples
juice of 1 lemon
2 teaspoons caraway seeds
For the dressing
¼ cup olive oil
1 tablespoon cider vinegar
1 teaspoon honey
salt and ground black pepper

1   Finely shred all the cabbages and place the shredded cabbage in a large salad bowl.

2   Chop the dates and add them to the cabbage.

3   Core the apples and slice them thinly into a mixing bowl. Add the lemon juice and toss together to prevent discoloration before adding them to the salad bowl.

4   Make the dressing. Combine the oil, vinegar and honey in a screw-top jar. Add salt and pepper, then close the jar tightly and shake well. Pour the dressing over the salad, toss lightly, then sprinkle with the caraway seeds and toss again.

COOK'S TIPS
Support local orchards by looking for different homegrown apples. Many delicious older "heirloom" varieties are grown by local farmers, who will willingly offer a taste to would-be buyers. Choose both green and red-skinned apples if possible, to add extra color to the salad.

SPROUTED SEED SALAD

If you sprout beans, lentils and whole grains, this increases their nutritional value, and they make a deliciously crunchy salad.

Preparation time 5 minutes
Cooking time None

SERVES 4

2 eating apples
2 cups alfalfa sprouts
2 cups bean sprouts
2 cups aduki bean sprouts
¼ cucumber, sliced
1 bunch watercress, trimmed
For the dressing
⅔ cup low-fat plain yogurt
juice of ½ lemon
bunch of chives, snipped
2 tablespoons chopped fresh herbs
ground black pepper

1   Core and slice the apples; mix with the other salad ingredients.

2   Whisk the dressing ingredients in a cup. Drizzle over the salad and toss together just before serving.

COOK'S TIP
You'll find a variety of bean and seed sprouts in the refrigerated section of large supermarkets and health food stores. They are best used the day that you buy them, but will keep in the vegetable bin of your refrigerator for a day or two.

Citrus Green Leaf Salad with Croutons

Whole-wheat croutons add a delicious crunch to green salads. The kumquats or orange segments provide a color contrast as well as a good helping of vitamin C.

Preparation time 4 minutes
Cooking time 1 minute

Serves 4–6

4 kumquats or 2 seedless oranges
7 ounces mixed salad greens
4 slices of whole-wheat bread,
  crusts removed
2–3 tablespoons pine nuts,
  lightly toasted
For the dressing
grated rind of 1 lemon
1 tablespoon lemon juice
3 tablespoons olive oil
1 teaspoon whole-grain mustard
1 garlic clove, crushed
salt and ground black pepper

1 Thinly slice the kumquats, or peel and segment the oranges.

> #### Cook's Tip
> Kumquats look like tiny oval oranges. The skin is edible.

2 Tear all the salad greens into bite-size pieces and mix together in a large salad bowl.

3 Toast the bread on both sides and cut into cubes. Add to the salad greens with the sliced kumquats or orange segments.

4 Shake all the dressing ingredients together in a jar. Pour over the salad just before serving and sprinkle the toasted pine nuts over the top.

Mixed Bean Salad with Tomato Dressing

All beans are a good source of vegetable protein and minerals; this hearty salad makes a meal.

Preparation time 3–4 minutes
Cooking time 5–6 minutes

Serves 4

4 ounces green beans
15-ounces canned mixed beans,
  drained, rinsed and drained again
2 celery ribs, finely chopped
1 small onion, finely chopped
3 tomatoes, chopped
chopped fresh parsley, to garnish
For the dressing
3 tablespoons olive oil
2 teaspoons red wine vinegar
1 garlic clove, crushed
1 tablespoon tomato chutney
salt and ground black pepper

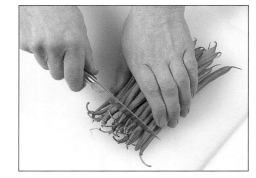

1 Remove the ends from the green beans, then cook them in boiling water for 5–6 minutes, until tender. Drain, refresh under cold running water, drain again and cut into thirds.

2 Place all the beans in a large bowl. Add the celery, onion and tomatoes and toss to mix.

3 Shake the dressing ingredients together in a jar. Pour over the salad and sprinkle with the parsley.

> #### Cook's Tip
> Using canned beans saves the hassle of long soaking and cooking that dried beans require. Try mixing several different types, such as chickpeas, pinto, black-eye, red kidney, soy and aduki beans.

SPINACH WITH RAISINS AND PINE NUTS

Raisins and pine nuts are frequent partners in Spanish recipes. Here, tossed with wilted spinach and croutons, they make a delicious and swiftly prepared salad.

Preparation time 2 minutes
Cooking time 5 minutes

SERVES 4
⅓ cup raisins
1 thick slice crusty white bread
3 tablespoons olive oil
⅓ cup pine nuts
1¼ pounds young spinach leaves, stalks removed
2 garlic cloves, crushed
salt and ground black pepper

1 Put the raisins in a small bowl. Pour over boiling water to cover and let soak while you make the croutons and prepare the rest of the salad ingredients.

2 Cut the bread into cubes and discard the crusts. Heat 2 tablespoons of the oil and sauté the bread until golden. Drain.

3 Heat the remaining oil in the pan. Sauté the pine nuts until beginning to color. Add the spinach and garlic and cook quickly, turning the spinach until it has just wilted.

4 Drain the raisins and add them to the pan. Toss gently and season lightly with salt and pepper. Transfer to a warmed serving dish. Sprinkle with the croutons and serve the salad at once.

VARIATIONS
When you have a little more time, use green or red Swiss chard instead of the spinach. They need to be cooked for slightly longer, but both have very good flavor.

Balti Mushrooms in a Creamy Garlic Sauce

This simple and delicious recipe could be served on whole-wheat toast or with basmati rice.

Preparation time 5 minutes
Cooking time 5 minutes

Serves 4

12 ounces (3 cups) button mushrooms
3 tablespoons olive oil
1 bay leaf
3 garlic cloves, roughly chopped
2 green chiles, seeded and chopped
1 cup fromage frais
1 tablespoon chopped fresh mint
1 tablespoon chopped cilantro
1 teaspoon salt
fresh mint and cilantro leaves,
  to garnish

1 Unless they are very small, cut the mushrooms in half. Set them aside in a bowl.

2 Heat the oil in a nonstick wok or large frying pan, then add the bay leaf, garlic and chiles and cook for about 1 minute.

3 Add the mushrooms. Stir-fry for about 2 minutes.

Cook's Tip
Cook the mushrooms for longer if you like them well cooked and browned.

4 Remove from the heat and stir in the fromage frais, followed by the mint, cilantro and salt. Heat, stirring, for 2 minutes, then transfer to a warmed serving dish, garnish with the mint and cilantro leaves and serve at once.

VEGETABLE AND EGG NOODLE RIBBONS

Serve this elegant, colorful dish with a tossed green salad as a light lunch. Use fresh pasta for optimum speed and flavor.

Preparation time 3 minutes
Cooking time 7 minutes

SERVES 4

1 large carrot, peeled
2 zucchini
4 tablespoons butter
1 tablespoon olive oil
6 fresh shiitake mushrooms, finely sliced
1/2 cup frozen peas, thawed
12 ounces broad egg noodles
2 teaspoons chopped fresh mixed herbs, such as marjoram, chives and basil
salt and ground black pepper
1 ounce Parmesan cheese (1/4 cup grated), to serve (optional)

1 Using a vegetable peeler, carefully slice the carrot and the zucchini into thin strips.

2 Heat the butter with the olive oil in a large frying pan. Stir in the carrots and shiitake mushrooms; cook for 2 minutes. Add the zucchini and peas and stir-fry until the zucchini are cooked but still crisp. Season with salt and pepper.

3 Meanwhile, cook the noodles in a large saucepan of boiling water until just tender. Drain the noodles well and pour them into a bowl. Add the vegetables and toss gently to mix.

4 Sprinkle on the fresh herbs and season to taste. If using the Parmesan cheese, grate or shave it over the top. Toss lightly and serve.

BUCKWHEAT NOODLES WITH GOAT CHEESE

When you don't feel like doing a lot of cooking, try this good, fast supper dish. The earthy flavor of buckwheat goes well with the nutty, peppery taste of arugula leaves, and both are offset by the deliciously creamy goat cheese.

Preparation and cooking time 8–10 minutes

SERVES 4

12 ounces buckwheat noodles
4 tablespoons butter
2 garlic cloves, finely chopped
4 shallots, sliced
3/4 cup hazelnuts, lightly roasted and roughly chopped
large handful arugula leaves
6 ounces goat cheese
salt and ground black pepper

1 Bring a large saucepan of lightly salted water to a rolling boil and add the noodles. Cook until just tender.

2 Meanwhile, heat the butter in a large frying pan. Add the garlic and shallots and cook for 2–3 minutes, stirring all the time, until the shallots are soft. Do not let the garlic brown.

3 Drain the noodles well. Add the hazelnuts to the pan and cook for about 1 minute. Add the arugula leaves and, when they start to wilt, toss in the noodles and heat through.

4 Season with salt and pepper. Crumble in the goat cheese and serve immediately.

MELON AND STRAWBERRY SALAD

A beautiful and colorful fruit salad, this is a particularly good dessert to serve after a spicy main course. For speed, cube the melons.

Preparation time 8–10 minutes
Cooking time None

Serves 4
1 Galia melon
1 honeydew melon
1/2 watermelon
2 cups fresh strawberries
1 tablespoon lemon juice
1 tablespoon honey
1 tablespoon water
1 tablespoon chopped fresh mint
1 mint sprig, to garnish (optional)

1 Prepare the melons by cutting them in half and discarding the seeds. Use a melon baller to scoop out the flesh in balls, or cut it into cubes with a knife. Place the melon balls (or cubes) in a fruit bowl.

2 Rinse and take the stems off the strawberries, cut them in half and add them to the fruit bowl.

3 Mix together the lemon juice, honey and water. Stir carefully to blend and then pour over the fruit. Stir the fruit so that it is thoroughly coated in the lemon and honey mixture.

4 Sprinkle the chopped mint over the top of the fruit. Serve garnished with the mint sprig, if you like.

COOK'S TIP
Use whichever melons are available: Substitute cantaloupe for Galia or Charentais for watermelon, for example. However, try to find three different kinds of melon so that you get variation in color, and also a variety of textures and flavors.

FIGS WITH RICOTTA CREAM

Fresh, ripe figs are full of natural sweetness and need little adornment. This simple recipe makes the most of their beautiful, intense flavor.

Preparation time 3–4 minutes
Cooking time None

SERVES 4
4 ripe, fresh figs
½ cup ricotta or
   cottage cheese
3 tablespoons crème fraîche
1 tablespoon honey
½ teaspoon pure vanilla extract
freshly grated nutmeg, to decorate

1   Trim the stems from the figs. Make four cuts through each fig from the stem end, cutting them almost through but leaving them joined at the base.

3   Mix together the ricotta or cottage cheese, crème fraîche, honey and vanilla extract.

4   Spoon a little ricotta cream onto to each plate and sprinkle with grated nutmeg to serve.

2   Place the figs on serving plates and ease the cuts apart gently to open them out.

VARIATION
Use full-fat soft cheese instead of ricotta or cottage cheese and strained plain yogurt in place of the crème fraîche.

EMERALD FRUIT SALAD

The cool, green-colored fruits make a refreshing—and fast—dessert.

Preparation and cooking time 8 minutes

SERVES 4
2 tablespoons lime juice
2 tablespoons honey
2 green eating apples, cored and sliced
1 small ripe green melon, diced
2 kiwifruit, sliced
1 star fruit, sliced
fresh mint sprigs, to decorate
yogurt or fromage frais, to serve

1 Mix together the lime juice and honey in a large bowl, then toss the apple slices in this.

2 Stir in the melon, kiwifruit and star fruit. Place in a glass serving dish.

3 Decorate the fruit salad with mint sprigs and serve with yogurt or fromage frais.

VARIATIONS

Add other green fruits when available, such as greengages, grapes, pears or horned melon. It has a tough yellowy orange rind covered with sharp spikes, and the flesh inside looks like a bright green jelly, encasing edible seeds that can be removed with a spoon. If time permits, chill the salad for an hour or two before serving. It is delicious with extra-thick cream to which a couple of spoonfuls of advocaat or eggnog have been added.

WARM BAGELS WITH POACHED APRICOTS

Preparation time 2 minutes
Cooking time 8 minutes

SERVES 4

a few strips of orange zest
1¹⁄₃ cups dried apricots
1 cup orange juice
¹⁄₂ teaspoon orange flower water
2 cinnamon and raisin bagels
4 teaspoons orange marmalade
4 tablespoons crème fraîche or
*   sour cream*
2 tablespoons chopped pistachio
*   nuts, to decorate*

1　Cut the strips of orange zest into fine shreds. Cook them in boiling water until softened, then drain and place in cold water.

2　Preheat the oven to 325°F. Combine the apricots and orange juice in a small saucepan. Simmer for about 6 minutes, until the juice has reduced and looks syrupy. Allow to cool, then stir in the orange flower water. Meanwhile, place the bagels on a baking sheet and warm in the oven for 5–10 minutes.

3　Split the bagels in half horizontally. Lay one half, cut side up, on each serving plate. Spread 1 teaspoon orange marmalade on each bagel.

4　Spoon 1 tablespoon crème fraîche or sour cream into the center of each bagel and place a quarter of the apricot compote at the side. Sprinkle orange zest and pistachio nuts over the top to decorate. Serve immediately.

COOK'S TIP
When you remove the strips of zest from the orange, use a swivel-action vegetable peeler to obtain thin strips and avoid removing any of the bitter white pith with the zest.

BRAZILIAN COFFEE BANANAS

Rich, lavish and sinful-looking, this is one of the fastest desserts: a must in the quick cook's repertoire.

Preparation time 4 minutes
Cooking time None

SERVES 4

4 small ripe bananas
1 tablespoon instant coffee granules
1 tablespoon hot water
2 tablespoons dark brown sugar
generous 1 cup strained plain yogurt
1 tablespoon toasted sliced almonds

1 Peel and slice one banana and mash the remaining three with a fork. Set the sliced banana aside.

2 Dissolve the coffee granules in the hot water and stir into the mashed bananas.

3 Spoon a little of the mashed banana mixture into four serving dishes and sprinkle with the brown sugar. Top with a spoonful of yogurt, then repeat until all the ingredients are used up.

4 Swirl the last layer of yogurt for a marbled effect. Finish with a few banana slices and the sliced almonds. Serve immediately, or the bananas will discolor.

Hot Bananas with Rum and Raisins

Choose almost-ripe bananas with evenly colored skins, either all yellow or just green at the tips.

Preparation time 2 minutes
Cooking time 3–4 minutes

SERVES 4
¼ cup raisins
5 tablespoons dark rum
4 tablespoons unsalted butter
¼ cup light brown sugar
4 ripe bananas, peeled and halved
  lengthwise
¼ teaspoon grated nutmeg
¼ teaspoon ground cinnamon
2 tablespoons slivered almonds, toasted
chilled cream or vanilla ice cream,
  to serve (optional)

1 Put the raisins in a bowl with the rum. Let them soak while you sauté the bananas.

2 Melt the butter in a frying pan, add the sugar and stir until dissolved. Add the bananas and cook for a few minutes, until tender.

3 Sprinkle the spices over the bananas, then pour the rum and raisins on top. Carefully set alight using a long match and stir gently.

4 Sprinkle on the almonds and serve immediately with chilled cream or ice cream.

STRAWBERRY MERINGUE PUDDING

This dish, called Eton Mess, is enjoyed by parents and students picnicking on the lawns at Eton College's annual prize-giving in June. Chill the strawberries in kirsch if you have time.

Preparation time 7 minutes
Cooking time None

SERVES 4
5 cups strawberries, chopped
3–4 tablespoons kirsch
1¼ cups heavy cream
6 small white meringues
fresh mint sprigs, to decorate

1 Put the strawberries in a bowl, sprinkle with the kirsch, then set aside for 3–4 minutes.

2 Whip the cream until soft peaks form, then gently fold in the strawberries with their juices.

3 Crush the meringues into rough chunks, then sprinkle over the strawberry mixture and fold in gently.

4 Spoon the strawberry mixture into a glass serving bowl, decorate with mint sprigs and serve immediately.

COOK'S TIP
If you would prefer to make a less rich version, use strained plain yogurt or thick plain yogurt instead of part or all of the cream. Simply beat the yogurt gently before adding the strawberry and kirsch mixture.

ICE CREAM STRAWBERRY SHORTCAKE

This dessert is an American classic, and couldn't be easier to make. Fresh juicy strawberries, store-bought sponge tart shells and rich ice cream are all you need to create a delicious dessert.

Preparation time 10 minutes
Cooking time None

SERVES 4
*3 x 6-inch sponge tart shells
   or shortbreads
6 cups strawberries
5 cups vanilla or strawberry ice
   cream
confectioners' sugar, for dusting*

1   If using sponge tart shells, trim the raised edges with a serrated knife.

2   Hull and halve the strawberries. Spoon one-third of the ice cream onto a tart shell or shortbread layer, placing it in scoops, with one-third of the strawberries in between.

3   Spoon more strawberries and ice cream onto a second tart or shortbread layer and place it on top of the first, then add the final layer, piling the strawberries up high.

COOK'S TIPS
Don't worry if the shortcake falls apart a little when you cut into it. It may look messy, but it will taste marvelous. If time permits, the dessert can be assembled up to an hour before serving and kept in the freezer without spoiling the fruit.

MANDARINS IN ORANGE FLOWER SYRUP

You can cheat with this recipe and buy canned whole peeled mandarins or clementines. Use fresh orange juice for the syrup. You can serve the dessert as soon as you make it, but it is even better chilled.

Preparation time 10 minutes
Cooking time None

SERVES 4
10 mandarins
1 tablespoon confectioners' sugar
2 teaspoon orange flower water
1 tablespoon chopped pistachio nuts

1 Thinly pare a little of the colored zest from one mandarin and cut it into fine shreds for decoration. Squeeze the juice from two mandarins and reserve it.

2 Peel the remaining fruit, removing as much of the white pith as possible. Arrange the whole fruit in a wide dish.

3 Mix the reserved juice, confectioners' sugar and orange flower water and pour it over the fruit. Cover the dish and chill for 5 minutes.

4 Meanwhile, blanch the shreds of zest in boiling water for 30 seconds. Drain and let cool. Sprinkle them over the mandarins with the pistachio nuts to serve.

PAPAYA SKEWERS WITH PASSION FRUIT COULIS

Fresh-tasting tropical fruits, full of natural sweetness, make a simple, exotic dessert.

Preparation time 7–8 minutes
Cooking time None

SERVES 6
3 ripe papayas
10 passion fruit or kiwifruit
2 tablespoons lime juice
2 tablespoons confectioners' sugar
2 tablespoons white rum
lime slices, to decorate

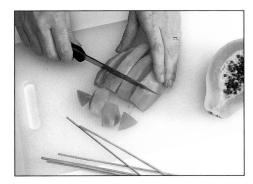

1 Cut the papayas in half and scoop out the seeds. Peel them and cut the flesh into even-size chunks. Thread the chunks onto six bamboo skewers.

2 Cut eight of the passion fruit in half and scoop out the flesh with a teaspoon. Purée the flesh for a few seconds in a blender or food processor. If using kiwifruit, slice off the top and bottom from eight of the fruits, then remove the skin. Cut the kiwifruit in half and purée them briefly.

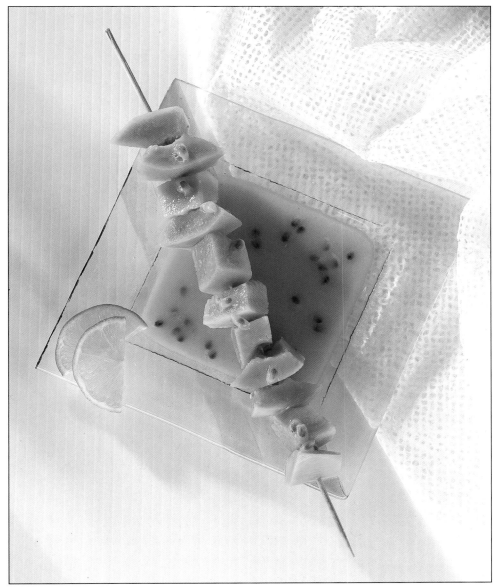

3 Press the pulp through a sieve placed over a bowl and discard the seeds. Add the lime juice, confectioners' sugar and rum, and stir until the sugar has dissolved.

4 Spoon a little coulis onto six serving plates. Arrange the skewers on top. Scoop the flesh from the remaining passion fruit and spoon it on or slice the kiwifruit and add it. Decorate with the lime slices.

COOK'S TIP
If you are short of time, the passion fruit flesh can be used as it is, without puréeing or sieving. Simply scoop the flesh from the skins and mix it with the lime, sugar and rum. Kiwifruit will still need to be puréed, however.

Quick Apricot Blender Whip

This is one of the quickest desserts you could make—and also one of the prettiest.

Preparation time 4 minutes
Cooking time 2 minutes

SERVES 4
14-ounce can apricot halves in juice
1 tablespoon Grand Marnier
   or brandy
¾ cup strained plain yogurt
2 tablespoons sliced almonds

COOK'S TIP
For an even lighter dessert, use low-fat instead of thick, creamy yogurt, and, if you prefer to omit the liqueur, add a little of the fruit juice from the can.

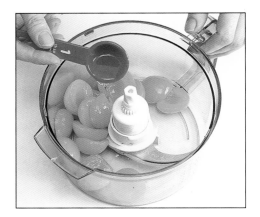

1 Drain the juice from the apricots and place the fruit in a blender or food processor with the liqueur.

2 Process the apricots until they are smooth.

3 Spoon the fruit purée and yogurt in alternate spoonfuls into four tall glasses or glass dishes, swirling them together slightly to give a marbled effect.

4 Lightly toast the almonds until they are golden. Let them cool slightly and then sprinkle some on top of each dessert.

RASPBERRY AND PASSION FRUIT SWIRLS

If passion fruit is not available, just use extra raspberries.

Preparation time 4–5 minutes
Cooking time None

SERVES 4
2 cups raspberries
2 passion fruit
1¾ cups low-fat fromage frais
2 tablespoons sugar
raspberries and sprigs of mint,
  to decorate

1 Mash the raspberries in a small bowl with a fork until the juice runs. Scoop out the passion fruit pulp into a separate bowl, and mix in the fromage frais and sugar.

2 Spoon alternate spoonfuls of the raspberry pulp and the fromage frais mixture into stemmed glasses or one large serving dish, stirring lightly to create a gentle swirled effect.

3 Decorate each dessert with a whole raspberry and a sprig of fresh mint. Serve at once.

COOK'S TIP
Overripe, slightly soft fruit can also be used in this recipe. You could use frozen raspberries when fresh are not available, but thaw them first.

VARIATION
Other summer fruits could be used—try a mix of strawberries and red currants with the raspberries, or use peeled and pitted mangoes, peaches or apricots, which you will need to purée in a food processor or blender before mixing with the fromage frais.

ITALIAN RICOTTA PUDDING

This creamy, rich dessert is very easy to make. Ideally, it should be chilled before serving (and can be made up to 24 hours ahead) but it can be served within minutes of making. Just pop it in the freezer while you eat your main course.

Preparation time 5–6 minutes
Cooking time None

SERVES 4–6
1 cup ricotta cheese
⅓ cup candied fruits
¼ cup sweet Marsala
1 cup heavy cream
¼ cup superfine sugar, plus extra to serve
finely grated rind of 1 orange
2 cups fresh raspberries
strips of thinly pared orange zest, to decorate

1. Press the ricotta through a sieve into a bowl. Finely chop the candied fruits and stir into the sieved ricotta with half the Marsala. Put the cream, sugar and orange zest in another bowl and whip until the cream is standing in soft peaks.

2. Fold the whipped cream into the ricotta mixture. Spoon into individual glass serving bowls and top with the raspberries.

3. Sprinkle the raspberries with the remaining Marsala and dust the top of each dessert liberally with sugar. Decorate with the strips of pared orange zest and serve.

COOK'S TIP
Buy candied fruits in large pieces from a good delicatessen—tubs of chopped candied peel are too tough to eat raw, and should only be used in baking.

CHOCOLATE FUDGE SUNDAES

Preparation time 3 minutes
Cooking time 6 minutes

SERVES 4

*4 scoops each vanilla and coffee
   ice cream*
2 small ripe bananas, sliced
whipped cream
toasted sliced almonds
For the sauce
⅓ cup light brown sugar
½ cup golden syrup or light corn syrup
3 tablespoons strong black coffee
1 teaspoon ground cinnamon
5 ounces semisweet chocolate, chopped
⅓ cup whipping cream
3 tablespoons coffee liqueur (optional)

1 To make the sauce, place the sugar, syrup, coffee and cinnamon in a heavy saucepan. Bring to a boil, then boil for about 5 minutes, stirring.

2 Turn off the heat, let cool for 1 minute, then stir in the chopped chocolate. When melted and smooth, stir in the cream and liqueur, if using. Let cool slightly while you assemble the sundaes.

3 Fill four tall glasses with a small scoop each of vanilla and coffee ice cream.

4 Scatter the sliced bananas over the ice cream. Pour the warm fudge sauce over the bananas, then top each sundae with a generous swirl of whipped cream. Sprinkle with toasted sliced almonds and serve at once.

VARIATIONS

Vary the taste of this dessert by choosing other flavors of ice cream. Strawberry, toffee or chocolate work well. In the summer, substitute raspberries or strawberries for the bananas, and sprinkle chopped roasted hazelnuts on top in place of the almonds.

20-MINUTE RECIPES

It may surprise you to find just how many delicious dishes can be prepared in twenty minutes. In less time than it takes to reheat a frozen meal, you can impress your guests with Poached Eggs with Spinach or Pan-steamed Mussels with Thai Herbs. Pasta really is faster these days, with fresh and quick-cooking varieties readily available, so celebrate with Tagliatelle with Tomatoes and Black Olives. For a final flourish, try Apple Soufflé Omelet or Orange Yogurt Brûlée.

Fresh Tomato Soup with Cheese Croûtes

Intensely flavored sun-ripened tomatoes need little embellishment in this fresh-tasting soup. If you buy from the supermarket, choose the ripest-looking ones and adjust the amount of sugar and vinegar, depending on the tomatoes' natural sweetness. On a hot day, this Italian soup is also delicious chilled.

Preparation time 5 minutes
Cooking time 13–14 minutes

Serves 6

3–3 ½ pounds ripe tomatoes
1 ²/₃ cups chicken or vegetable stock
3 tablespoons sun-dried tomato paste
2–3 tablespoons balsamic vinegar
2–3 teaspoons sugar
small handful fresh basil leaves, plus a few extra to garnish
salt and ground black pepper
toasted cheese croûtes and crème fraîche, to serve

1. Mark the tomatoes with a small cross at the base, plunge them into boiling water for 30 seconds, then refresh in cold water. Peel away the skins and quarter the tomatoes. Put them in a large saucepan and pour the chicken or vegetable stock over them. Bring just to a boil, reduce the heat, cover and simmer gently for about 10 minutes, or until all the tomatoes are pulpy.

2. Stir in the tomato paste, vinegar, sugar and basil. Season with salt and pepper, then cook gently, stirring, for 2 minutes.

3. Process the soup in a blender or food processor, then return to the pan and reheat gently.

4. Serve in heated bowls. Top each portion with one or two toasted cheese croûtes and a spoonful of crème fraîche, garnished with the basil leaves.

Cook's Tips
Use good-quality stock for this soup. If you don't have time to make your own stock—or feel that life's too short for such worthy pursuits—buy superior canned stock.

RED PEPPER SOUP WITH CHILE AND LIME

The beautiful rich red color of this soup makes it a very attractive first course or light lunch.

Preparation and cooking time 20 minutes

SERVES 4–6
4 red bell peppers, seeded and chopped
1 large onion, chopped
1 teaspoon olive oil
1 garlic clove, crushed
1 small red chile, seeded and sliced
3 tablespoons tomato paste
3 ¾ cups chicken stock
finely grated zest and juice of 1 lime
salt and ground black pepper
shreds of lime zest, to garnish

1. Cook the peppers and onion gently in the oil in a covered saucepan for about 5 minutes, shaking the pan occasionally.

2. Stir in the garlic, then add the chile with the tomato paste. Stir in half the stock, then bring to a boil. Cover the pan, lower the heat and simmer for 10 minutes.

3. Purée the mixture in a food processor or blender. Return to the pan, then add the rest of the stock.

4. Add the grated lime zest and juice to the soup, with salt and pepper to taste. Bring the soup back to a boil, then serve at once with strips of lime zest scattered into each bowl.

COOK'S TIPS

Yellow or orange bell peppers could be substituted for the red bell peppers. If you haven't got a fresh chile (or don't have time to seed and slice one), add a dash or two of Tabasco sauce to the soup instead.

SPANISH GARLIC SOUP

This is a simple and satisfying soup, made with one of the most popular ingredients in the quick cook's kitchen—garlic!

Preparation time 2 minutes
Cooking time 12 minutes

SERVES 4

2 tablespoons olive oil
4 large garlic cloves, peeled
4 slices French bread, about
    ¼ inch thick
1 tablespoon paprika
4 cups beef stock
¼ teaspoon ground cumin
pinch of saffron strands
4 eggs
salt and ground black pepper
chopped fresh parsley, to garnish

1 Preheat the oven to 450°F. Heat the oil in a large pan. Add the whole garlic cloves and cook until golden. Remove and set aside. Sauté the bread in the oil until golden, then set aside.

2 Add the paprika to the pan and sauté for a few seconds. Stir in the beef stock, cumin and saffron, then add the reserved garlic, crushing the cloves with the back of a wooden spoon. Season with salt and pepper, then cook for about 5 minutes.

3 Ladle the soup into four ovenproof bowls and break an egg into each. Place a slice of fried bread on top of each egg, then put the bowls in the oven for 3–4 minutes, until the eggs are set. Sprinkle each portion with parsley and serve at once.

COOK'S TIP

When you turn the oven on, put in a baking sheet at the same time. Stand the soup bowls on the hot baking sheet when you put them in the oven and you will be able to remove them quickly and easily as soon as the eggs have set.

FRESH PEA SOUP

You really need fresh peas for this soup, but shelling them can be time-consuming. Delegate the job to young kitchen hands if you can, or use frozen peas, thawing and rinsing them before use.

Preparation time 2–5 minutes
Cooking time 15 minutes

SERVES 2–3
small pat of butter
2 or 3 shallots, finely chopped
3 cups shelled fresh peas (from about
*   3 pounds garden peas) or thawed*
*   frozen peas*
2 cups water
3–4 tablespoons whipping cream
*   (optional)*
salt and ground black pepper
croutons or crumbled crisp bacon,
*   to garnish*

1 Melt the butter in a heavy saucepan or flameproof casserole. Add the shallots and cook for about 3 minutes, stirring occasionally.

COOK'S TIP
If you use frozen peas for the soup, cook them in flavorful vegetable stock or light chicken stock instead of water, because they will lack the delicate flavor of freshly shelled garden peas. Instead of stirring the cream into the soup, swirl it on top when serving.

2 Add the peas and water and season with salt and a little pepper. Cover and simmer for about 12 minutes for young or frozen peas and up to 15 minutes for large or older peas, stirring occasionally.

3 When the peas are tender, ladle them into a food processor or blender with a little of the cooking liquid and process until smooth.

4 Strain the pea soup into the saucepan or casserole, stir in the cream, if using, and heat through without boiling. Add seasoning and serve hot, garnished with croutons or bacon.

HADDOCK AND BROCCOLI CHOWDER

A warming main-dish soup for hearty appetites.

Preparation time 5 minutes
Cooking time 15 minutes

SERVES 4
4 scallions, sliced
1 pound new potatoes, diced
1¼ cups water
1¼ cups milk
1 bay leaf
2 cups broccoli florets, sliced
1 pound smoked haddock
   fillets, skinned
7-ounce can corn, drained
ground black pepper
chopped scallions, to garnish

1 Place the scallions and potatoes in a large saucepan and add the water, milk and bay leaf. Bring the liquid to a boil, then cover the pan, lower the heat and simmer for 8 minutes.

2 Add the broccoli. Cut the fish into bite-size chunks and place in the pan with the corn.

3 Season the mixture well with black pepper, then cover the pan and simmer for 5 minutes more, or until the fish is cooked through. Remove the bay leaf and sprinkle the scallions over the top. Serve the soup hot, with crusty bread.

COOK'S TIP
New potatoes are now available for most of the year.

VARIATIONS
Smoked cod fillets would be equally good in this chowder, or, if you prefer, substitute white cod or haddock fillets for half or all of the smoked fish.

CORN AND CRAB CHOWDER

The name chowder comes from the French word meaning a large cooking pot, which the fishermen on the east coast of North America used for boiling up whatever was left over from the sale of their catch for supper.

Preparation time 5 minutes
Cooking time 14 minutes

SERVES 4

2 tablespoons butter
1 small onion, chopped
12-ounce can corn, drained
2½ cups milk
6-ounce can crabmeat, drained and flaked
1 cup peeled, cooked shrimp
2 scallions, finely chopped
⅔ cup light cream or creamy milk
pinch of cayenne pepper
salt and ground black pepper
4 cooked shrimp in shells, to garnish

1 Melt the butter in a large saucepan and gently sauté the onion for 4–5 minutes, until softened.

2 Reserve 2 tablespoons of the corn for the garnish and add the remainder to the pan with the milk. Bring the milk to a boil, then lower the heat, cover the pan and simmer, stirring occasionally, for 5 minutes.

3 Pour the corn mixture, in batches if necessary, into a blender or food processor and blend until smooth.

4 Return the mixture to the pan and stir in the crabmeat, shrimp, scallions, cream or milk and cayenne pepper. Reheat gently.

5 Meanwhile, place the reserved corn kernels in a small frying pan without oil and dry-fry over medium heat until golden and toasted. Season the soup well and serve each bowlful topped with a few of the toasted kernels and a whole shrimp.

CHILE BEEF NACHOS

The addition of ground beef to this traditional appetizer demonstrates the use of hamburger as an excellent extender, creating a filling meal.

Preparation time 3–4 minutes
Cooking time 14–15 minutes

SERVES 4
1 cup ground beef
2 red chiles, chopped
3 scallions, chopped
6 ounces tortilla chips
1¼ cups sour cream
½ cup freshly grated Cheddar cheese
salt and ground black pepper

1 Dry-fry the ground beef and chiles in a large pan for about 10 minutes, stirring all the time.

2 Add the scallions, season well and cook for another 2 minutes. Preheat the broiler.

3 Arrange the chips in four individual flameproof dishes.

4 Spoon on the ground beef mixture, top with dollops of sour cream and sprinkle with the grated cheese. Broil under medium heat for 2–3 minutes, or until the cheese is bubbling. Serve at once.

BREADED SOLE BATONS

Crisp, crumbed strips of fish—
an elegant, speedy preparation.

Preparation time 10–12 minutes
Cooking time 6–7 minutes

SERVES 4
10 ounces lemon sole fillets, skinned
2 eggs
2 cups fine fresh bread crumbs
³/₄ cup all-purpose flour
salt and ground black pepper
oil, for frying
lemon wedges and tartar sauce,
to serve

1 Cut the fish fillets into long diagonal strips, each measuring about ³/₄ inch wide.

2 Break the eggs into a shallow dish and beat well with a fork. Place the bread crumbs in another shallow dish. Put the flour in a large plastic bag and season with salt and ground black pepper.

3 Dip the fish strips in the egg, turning to coat well. Place on a plate and then shake a few at a time in the bag of seasoned flour. Dip the fish strips in the egg again and then in the bread crumbs, turning to coat well. Place on a baking sheet in a single layer, not touching. Let the coating set for at least 5 minutes.

4 Heat ¹/₂ inch oil in a large frying pan over medium-high heat. When the oil is hot (a cube of bread will sizzle) fry the fish strips in batches for 2–2¹/₂ minutes, turning once, taking care not to overcrowd the pan. Drain on paper towels and keep warm. Serve the fish with tartar sauce and lemon wedges.

SMOKED MACKEREL AND APPLE DIP

This quick fish dip is served with tasty curried toast.

Preparation time 5 minutes
Cooking time 10 minutes

SERVES 6–8
12 ounces smoked mackerel, skinned and boned
1 soft eating apple, peeled, cored and cut into chunks
⅔ cup fromage frais
pinch of paprika or curry powder
salt and ground black pepper
apple slices, to garnish
For the toast
2 tablespoons butter, softened
1 teaspoon curry paste
4 slices white bread, crusts removed

1 Place the smoked mackerel in a food processor with the apple, fromage frais and seasonings.

2 Blend for about 2 minutes, or until the mixture is very smooth. Check the seasoning, then transfer to a small serving dish.

3 Preheat the oven to 400ºF. To make the toast, place the bread on a baking sheet. Blend the butter and curry paste; then spread over the bread.

4 Bake the bread for about 10 minutes, or until crisp and golden. Cut into strips and serve immediately, with the mackerel dip, garnished with the apple slices.

COOK'S TIP
Instead of using plain sliced bread, try other breads for the toast—Italian ciabatta, whole-wheat, rye, or pita breads would be excellent.

BAKED EGGS WITH TARRAGON

Traditional gratin dishes or small ramekins are ideal for this recipe.

Preparation time 1 minute
Cooking time 10–11 minutes

SERVES 4
3 tablespoons butter
1/2 cup heavy cream
1–2 tablespoons chopped fresh tarragon
4 eggs
salt and ground black pepper
fresh tarragon sprigs, to garnish

1 Preheat the oven to 350°F. Lightly butter four small ovenproof dishes, then warm them in the oven briefly.

2 Gently warm the cream. Sprinkle some tarragon into each dish, then spoon in some cream.

3 Carefully break an egg into each of the prepared ovenproof dishes, season the eggs with salt and pepper and spoon a little more of the cream over each of the eggs.

4 Add a small pat of butter to each dish and place them in a roasting pan. Pour in hot water to come halfway up the sides of the dishes. Bake for 8–10 minutes, until the whites are just set and the yolks still soft. Garnish with tarragon.

POACHED EGGS WITH SPINACH

This classic dish can be served as an appetizer, but is also excellent for a light lunch or brunch.

Preparation time 2 minutes
Cooking time 12 minutes

SERVES 4
2 tablespoons butter
1 pound young spinach leaves
½ teaspoon vinegar
4 eggs
salt and ground black pepper
For the hollandaise sauce
12 tablespoons (1½ sticks) butter, cut
  into small pieces
2 egg yolks
1 tablespoon lemon juice
1 tablespoon water
salt and ground white pepper

COOK'S TIP
Hollandaise sauce is quick and easy to make in a blender or food processor. If you wish, you can make it an hour or two in advance and keep it warm in a wide-mouthed thermos.

1 To make the hollandaise sauce, melt the butter in a small saucepan over medium heat until it bubbles, then remove from the heat.

2 Put the egg yolks, lemon juice and water into a blender or food processor and blend. With the machine running, slowly pour in the hot butter in a thin stream. Stop pouring when you reach the milky solids at the bottom of the pan. When the sauce thickens, season and add more lemon juice if needed. Transfer the sauce to a bowl, cover and keep warm.

3 Melt the butter in a heavy frying pan over medium heat. Add the spinach and cook until wilted, stirring occasionally. Season and keep warm.

4 To poach the eggs, bring a medium pan of lightly salted water to a boil and add the vinegar. Break an egg into a saucer or cup and slide the egg into the water. Reduce the heat and simmer for a few minutes, until the white is set and the yolk is still soft. Remove with a slotted spoon and drain. Trim any untidy edges with scissors and keep warm. Cook the remaining eggs in the same way.

5 To serve, spoon the spinach onto warmed plates and make an indentation in each mound. Place the eggs on top and pour a little hollandaise sauce over them. Serve the remaining hollandaise separately.

ASPARAGUS WITH ORANGE SAUCE

The white asparagus grown in France is considered a delicacy by many, although it doesn't have the intense flavor of the green. White and large green spears are best peeled before cooking.

Preparation time 2–3 minutes
Cooking time 15 minutes

*4 tablespoons unsalted butter, diced
3 egg yolks
1 tablespoon cold water
1 tablespoon fresh lemon juice
grated zest and juice of
    1 unwaxed orange, plus extra
    shreds of orange zest,
    to garnish
salt and cayenne pepper to taste
30–36 thick asparagus spears*

1 Melt the butter in a small saucepan over low heat; do not boil. Skim off any foam and set the pan aside.

2 In a heatproof bowl set over a saucepan of barely simmering water or in the top of a double boiler, whisk together the egg yolks, water, lemon juice and 1 tablespoon of the orange juice. Season with salt. Place the saucepan or double boiler over very low heat and whisk constantly until the mixture begins to thicken and the whisk begins to leave tracks on the bottom of the pan. Remove the pan from the heat.

3 Whisk in the melted butter, drop by drop, until the sauce begins to thicken, then pour it in a little more quickly, leaving behind the milky solids at the bottom of the pan. Whisk in the orange zest and 2–4 tablespoons of the orange juice. Season with salt and cayenne and keep warm, stirring occasionally

4 Cut off the tough ends from the asparagus spears and trim to the same length. If peeling, hold each spear gently by the tip, then use a vegetable peeler to strip off the peel and scales from just below the tip to the end. Rinse in cold water.

5 Pour water to a depth of 2 inches into a large deep frying pan or wok and bring to a boil over medium-high heat. Add the asparagus and bring back to a boil, then simmer for 4–7 minutes, until just tender.

6 Carefully transfer the spears to a large colander to drain, then lay them on a dish towel; pat dry. Arrange on a large serving platter or individual plates and spoon a little sauce over them. Sprinkle the orange zest over the sauce and serve at once.

COOK'S TIP
This sauce is a kind of hollandaise and needs gentle treatment. If the egg yolk mixture thickens too quickly, remove from the heat and plunge the bottom of the pan or bowl into cold water to prevent the sauce from curdling. The sauce should keep over hot water for 1 hour, but don't let it get too hot.

ASPARAGUS ROLLS WITH HERB BUTTER SAUCE

For a taste sensation, try tender asparagus spears wrapped in crisp phyllo pastry. The buttery herb sauce doesn't take long to make and is the perfect accompaniment.

Preparation time 5 minutes
Cooking time 8 minutes

SERVES 2
4 sheets of phyllo pastry
4 tablespoons butter, melted
16 young asparagus spears, trimmed
mixed salad, to garnish
For the sauce
2 shallots, finely chopped
1 bay leaf
²/₃ cup dry white wine
12 tablespoons (1½ sticks) butter, melted
1 tablespoon chopped fresh herbs
salt and ground black pepper
snipped chives, to garnish

1 Preheat the oven to 400°F. Grease a baking sheet. Brush each phyllo sheet with melted butter. Fold one corner of the sheet down to the bottom edge to give a wedge shape.

COOK'S TIPS
Make miniature asparagus rolls for parties. Cut smaller rectangles of phyllo and roll around single asparagus spears. Serve hot, with the suggested sauce, or cold, with a light mayonnaise. For a quicker and more economical version, use well-drained canned asparagus cuts, folding them inside phyllo envelopes.

2 Lay 4 asparagus spears on top at the longest edge and roll up toward the shortest edge. Using the remaining phyllo and asparagus spears, make 3 more rolls in the same way.

3 Lay the rolls on the prepared baking sheet. Brush with the remaining melted butter. Bake for 8 minutes, until golden.

4 Meanwhile, make the sauce. Put the shallots, bay leaf and wine in a pan. Cover and cook over high heat until the wine is reduced to 3–4 tablespoons.

5 Strain the wine mixture into a heatproof bowl. Whisk in the butter, a little at a time, until the sauce is smooth and glossy.

6 Stir in the herbs and add salt and pepper to taste. Keep the sauce warm over a pan of barely simmering water. Serve the rolls on individual plates with the salad garnish. Serve the butter sauce separately, sprinkled with a few snipped chives.

SALADE NIÇOISE

Preparation and
cooking time 20 minutes

SERVES 4

6 tablespoons olive oil
2 tablespoons tarragon vinegar
1 teaspoon tarragon or Dijon
   mustard
1 small garlic clove, crushed
4 ounces green beans
12 small new potatoes
3–4 romaine hearts
7-ounce can tuna in oil, drained
6 anchovy fillets, halved lengthwise
12 pitted black olives
4 tomatoes, chopped
4 scallions, finely chopped
2 teaspoons capers
2 tablespoons pine nuts
2 hard-boiled eggs, chopped

1 Mix the oil, vinegar, mustard,
garlic and seasoning with a
wooden spoon in a large salad bowl.

COOK'S TIP
When buying the potatoes, pick the
smallest ones you can find, so that they
cook quickly.

2 Cook the green beans and
potatoes in separate pans of
boiling salted water until just tender.
Drain and add to the bowl with the
lettuce, tuna, anchovies, olives,
tomatoes, scallions and capers.

3 Toast the pine nuts in a small
frying pan over medium heat
until lightly browned.

4 Sprinkle the pine nuts over the
salad while they are still hot,
add the chopped hard-boiled eggs
and toss all the ingredients together
well. Serve at once, with chunks of
hot crusty bread.

AVOCADO AND PAPAYA SALAD

Preparation time 6–8 minutes
Cooking time None

SERVES 4

2 ripe avocados
1 ripe papaya
1 large orange
1 small red onion
1–2 ounces small arugula leaves
For the dressing
¼ cup olive oil
2 tablespoons fresh lemon or lime juice
salt and ground black pepper

1. Halve the avocados and remove the pits. Carefully peel off the skin, then slice each avocado half thickly.

2. Peel the papaya. Cut it in half lengthwise and scoop out the seeds with a spoon. Set aside about 1 teaspoon of the seeds for the dressing. Cut each half into eight slices.

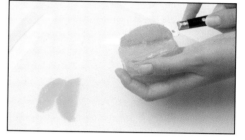

3. Peel the orange. Using a small, sharp knife, cut out the segments, cutting either side of the dividing membranes. Slice the onion thinly and separate into rings.

4. Make the dressing. Combine the oil, lemon or lime juice and seasoning in a bowl and mix well. Stir in the reserved papaya seeds.

5. Assemble the salad on four individual serving plates. Alternate slices of papaya and avocado. Add the orange segments and a mound of arugula or mâche topped with onion rings. Spoon on the dressing and serve.

CORNED BEEF HASH

This classic American hash, made with corned beef, is a popular brunch or lunchtime dish.

Preparation time 4 minutes
Cooking time 12–14 minutes

SERVES 4

2 tablespoons sunflower oil
2 tablespoons butter
1 onion, finely chopped
1 small green bell pepper, seeded
   and diced
2 large boiled potatoes, diced
12 ounces canned corned
   beef, cubed
¼ teaspoon grated nutmeg
¼ teaspoon paprika
4 eggs
salt and ground black pepper
chopped fresh parsley, to garnish
sweet chili sauce or tomato sauce,
   to serve

1. Heat the oil and butter together in a large frying pan and add the onion. Cook for 5–6 minutes, until softened.

2. In a bowl, mix together the pepper, potatoes, corned beef, nutmeg and paprika and season well. Add to the pan and toss gently. Press down lightly and cook over medium heat for 3–4 minutes, until a golden brown crust has formed on the bottom.

COOK'S TIP
Chill the corned beef before use—it will cut into cubes more easily.

3. Stir the hash mixture to distribute the crust, then repeat the frying twice, until the mixture is well browned.

4. Make four wells in the hash and crack an egg into each. Cover. Cook until the whites are just set.

5. Sprinkle with chopped parsley and cut the hash into quarters. Serve hot with sweet chili sauce or tomato sauce.

STILTON BURGERS

Rather more elegant than the traditional hamburger, this tasty recipe contains a delicious surprise. The lightly melted Stilton cheese encased in each crunchy burger is absolutely delicious.

Preparation time 5 minutes
Cooking time 10 minutes

SERVES 4
1 pound ground beef
1 onion, finely chopped
1 celery rib, chopped
1 teaspoon dried mixed herbs
1 teaspoon prepared mustard
$^1\!/_2$ cup crumbled blue
   Stilton cheese
4 hamburger buns
salt and ground black pepper

1 Place the ground beef in a bowl together with the onion and celery. Season well.

2 Stir in the herbs and mustard, bringing the mixture together to form a firm mixture.

3 Divide the mixture into eight equal portions. Place four on a cutting board and flatten each one slightly to make patties.

4 Place some crumbled cheese in the center of each patty.

5 Flatten the remaining mixture and place on top. Mold the mixture together, encasing the crumbled cheese, and shape into four neat hamburgers. Preheat the broiler.

6 Broil under medium heat for 10 minutes, turning once, or until cooked through. Split the buns and place a hamburger inside each. Serve with salad and relish or ketchup, if liked, although neither is essential with the Stilton for flavoring.

VEAL KIDNEYS WITH MUSTARD

In France, where this recipe originated, veal kidneys are generally used, but this dish is equally delicious made with lamb kidneys, if you can find them.

Preparation time 5 minutes
Cooking time 10–12 minutes

SERVES 4
2 veal kidneys or 8–10 lamb kidneys, trimmed and membranes removed
2 tablespoons butter
1 tablespoon vegetable oil
1 cup button mushrooms, quartered
¼ cup chicken stock
2 tablespoons brandy (optional)
¾ cup crème fraîche or heavy cream
2 tablespoons Dijon mustard
salt and ground black pepper
snipped fresh chives, to garnish

1 Cut the veal kidneys into pieces, discarding any fat. If using lamb kidneys, remove the central core by cutting a V shape from the middle of each kidney. Cut each kidney into three or four pieces.

COOK'S TIP
Be sure not to cook the sauce too long once the mustard is added, or it will lose its piquancy.

2 In a large frying pan, melt the butter with the oil over high heat and swirl to blend. Add the kidneys and sauté for 3–4 minutes, stirring frequently, until browned, then transfer them to a plate using a slotted spoon.

3 Add the mushrooms to the pan and sauté for 2–3 minutes, until golden, stirring frequently. Pour in the chicken stock and brandy, if using, then bring to a boil and boil for 2 minutes.

4 Lower the heat, stir in the crème fraîche or heavy cream and cook for 2–3 minutes, until the sauce is slightly thickened. Stir in the mustard and season with salt and pepper, then add the kidneys and cook for 1 minute to reheat. Spoon into a serving dish, sprinkle the chives over the kidneys and serve.

Beef Strips with Orange and Ginger

Stir-frying is one of the best ways to cook with a minimum of fat. It's also one of the quickest ways to cook, provided you choose tender meat.

Preparation time 15 minutes
Cooking time 5 minutes

Serves 4

1 pound lean beef steak, fillet or
  sirloin, cut into thin strips
grated zest and juice of 1 orange
1 tablespoon light soy sauce
1 teaspoon cornstarch
1-inch piece of fresh ginger root,
  finely chopped
1 tablespoon sunflower oil
1 large carrot, cut into thin strips
2 scallions, thinly sliced
noodles or rice, to serve

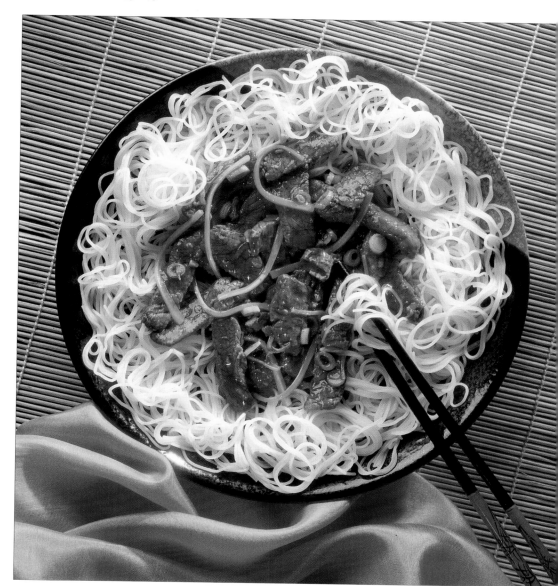

1   Place the beef strips in a bowl and sprinkle the orange zest and juice over them. If possible, let marinate for 10 minutes, or up to 30 minutes if you can spare the time.

2   Drain the liquid from the meat and set aside, then mix the meat with the soy sauce, cornstarch, and ginger.

Cook's Tip

Just before serving, toss the stir-fry with 1 teaspoon sesame oil. If you don't have sesame oil, use flavored chili oil, or a nut oil, such as hazelnut or walnut.

3   Heat the oil in a wok or large frying pan and add the beef. Stir-fry for 1 minute, until lightly colored, then add the carrot and stir-fry for 2–3 minutes more.

4   Stir in the scallions and reserved liquid, then cook, stirring, until boiling and thickened. Serve hot with noodles or rice.

RAGOUT OF VEAL

Full of flavor, this stew is quick and easy. Use small cubes of pork fillet if you prefer.

Preparation time 3 minutes
Cooking time 17 minutes

SERVES 4
1 pound veal tenderloin
2 tablespoons olive oil
10–12 tiny onions, kept whole
1 yellow bell pepper, seeded and cut
into eight pieces
1 orange or red bell pepper, seeded
and cut in eight
3 plum tomatoes, peeled and
quartered
4 sprigs of fresh basil
2 tablespoons dry vermouth or sherry
salt and ground black pepper

1 Trim off any fat and cut the veal into cubes. Heat the oil in a frying pan and gently sauté the veal and onions until browned.

2 After a couple of minutes, add the peppers and tomatoes. Sauté for another 4 minutes.

3 Add half the basil leaves, roughly chopped, the vermouth or sherry, and seasoning. Cook, stirring frequently, for 10 minutes, or until the meat is tender.

4 Sprinkle with the remaining basil leaves and serve hot.

LAMB'S LIVER WITH PEPPERS

Tender and tasty lamb's liver can be sautéed with all sorts of ingredients. Here it is matched with peppers and peppercorns.

Preparation time 7 minutes
Cooking time 3–4 minutes

SERVES 4
2 tablespoons olive oil
2 shallots, sliced
1 pound lamb's liver, cut into thin
strips
1 garlic clove, crushed
2 teaspoons green peppercorns,
crushed (or more to taste)
½ red bell pepper, seeded and cut
into strips
½ orange or yellow bell pepper,
seeded and cut into strips
2 tablespoons crème fraîche
salt and ground black pepper
rice or noodles, to serve

COOK'S TIP
Lamb's liver is best when still very slightly pink in the middle. Watch it closely, because it overcooks quickly.

1 Heat the oil and stir-fry the shallots briskly for 1 minute. Add the liver, garlic, peppercorns and peppers, then stir-fry for 3–4 minutes.

2 Stir in the crème fraîche, season to taste and serve immediately with rice or noodles.

TURKEY WITH YELLOW PEPPER SAUCE

Preparation time 6–8 minutes
Cooking time 12 minutes

SERVES 4

2 tablespoons olive oil
2 large yellow bell peppers, seeded
* and chopped*
1 small onion, chopped
1 tablespoon freshly squeezed
* orange juice*
1¼ cups chicken stock
4 turkey scallops
3 ounces Boursin or garlicky
* cream cheese*
16 fresh basil leaves
2 tablespoons butter
salt and ground black pepper

[1] To make the sauce, heat half the oil in a pan and gently sauté the peppers and onion until beginning to soften. Add the orange juice and stock and cook until very soft. Meanwhile, lay the turkey scallops between sheets of plastic wrap and pound them out lightly.

[2] Spread the turkey scallops with the Boursin or garlicky cream cheese. Chop half the basil and sprinkle on top, then roll up, tucking in the ends like an envelope. Secure with half a toothpick.

[3] Heat the remaining oil and the butter in a frying pan and sauté the scallops for 7–8 minutes, turning them frequently, until golden and cooked.

[4] While the scallops are cooking, press the pepper mixture through a sieve, or blend until smooth, then strain back into the pan. Season to taste and warm through, or serve cold, with the scallops, garnished with the remaining basil leaves.

COOK'S TIP
Chicken breast fillets or veal scallops could be used in place of the turkey, if you prefer.

COD WITH CAPER SAUCE

The quick and easy sauce with a slightly sharp and nutty flavor is a very effective way of enhancing this simple fish.

Preparation time 2 minutes
Cooking time 10 minutes

SERVES 4

4 cod steaks, about 6 ounces each
8 tablespoons (1 stick) butter
1 tablespoon small capers, rinsed,
  plus 1 tablespoon vinegar from the
  caper jar
1 tablespoon chopped fresh parsley
salt and ground black pepper
fresh tarragon sprigs, to garnish

1 Preheat the broiler. Season the cod. Melt 2 tablespoons of the butter, then brush some over one side of each piece of cod.

2 Broil the cod for 4 minutes, turn the fish over, then brush with melted butter and cook for another 4–5 minutes, or until the fish flakes easily.

3 Meanwhile, heat the remaining butter until it turns golden brown, then add the vinegar followed by the capers and stir well.

4 Pour the vinegar, butter and capers over the fish, sprinkle with parsley and garnish with the tarragon sprigs.

VARIATIONS
Thick tail fillets of cod or haddock could be used in place of the cod steaks. The sauce is also excellent with skate that has been panfried in butter.

TAGLIATELLE WITH SAFFRON MUSSELS

Preparation time 6 minutes
Cooking time 14 minutes

SERVES 4

4–4½ pounds live mussels
⅔ cup dry white wine
2 shallots, chopped
12 ounces fresh or dried tagliatelle
2 tablespoons butter
2 garlic cloves, crushed
1 cup heavy cream
generous pinch of saffron strands
1 egg yolk
salt and ground black pepper
2 tablespoons chopped fresh parsley,
  to garnish

1   Scrub the mussels well under cold running water. Remove the beards and discard any mussels that remain open when tapped.

2   Place the mussels in a large pan with the wine and shallots. Cover and cook over high heat, shaking occasionally, for 5–8 minutes, until the mussels have opened. Drain the mussels, reserving the liquid. Discard any mussels that remain closed. Shell most of the mussels; keep warm.

3   Bring the reserved cooking liquid to a boil, then reduce by half. Strain into a cup.

4   Cook the tagliatelle in a large pan of boiling salted water until just tender. Meanwhile, melt the butter in a separate pan and sauté the garlic for about a minute. Pour in the reserved mussel liquid, cream and saffron strands. Heat gently until the sauce thickens slightly. Remove the pan from the heat and stir in the egg yolk, shelled mussels and seasoning to taste.

5   Drain the tagliatelle, transfer to warmed serving bowls, then spoon the sauce on top and sprinkle with chopped parsley. Garnish with the mussels in shells. Serve at once.

COD CREOLE

Preparation time 5 minutes
Cooking time 10 minutes

SERVES 4

1 pound cod fillets, skinned
1 tablespoon lime or lemon juice
2 teaspoons olive oil
1 medium onion, finely chopped
1 green bell pepper, seeded and sliced
$\frac{1}{2}$ teaspoon cayenne pepper
$\frac{1}{2}$ teaspoon garlic salt
14-ounce can chopped tomatoes

COOK'S TIP

Be careful not to overcook the fish—or to let it bubble too vigorously in the sauce—or the chunks will break up. Test the fish frequently, and remove it from the heat the minute it is cooked.

1 Cut the cod fillets into bite-size chunks and sprinkle with the lime or lemon juice.

2 In a large pan, heat the olive oil and sauté the onion and pepper gently until softened. Add the cayenne pepper and garlic salt.

3 Stir in the cod chunks with the chopped tomatoes. Bring to a boil, then cover and simmer for about 5 minutes, or until the fish flakes easily when tested with the tip of a sharp knife. Serve with boiled rice or potatoes.

FIVE-SPICE FISH

Chinese mixtures of spicy, sweet and sour flavors are great with fish.

Preparation time 8 minutes
Cooking time 6 minutes

SERVES 4

4 white fish fillets, such as cod, haddock, or whiting, about 6 ounces each
1 teaspoon Chinese five-spice powder
4 teaspoons cornstarch
1 tablespoon sunflower oil
3 scallions, shredded
1 teaspoon grated fresh ginger root
$1\frac{1}{4}$ cups button mushrooms, sliced
$\frac{2}{3}$ cup baby corn, sliced
2 tablespoons soy sauce
3 tablespoons dry sherry
1 teaspoon sugar
salt and ground black pepper

1 Toss the fish in the five-spice powder and cornstarch to coat.

2 Heat the oil in a frying pan or wok and stir-fry the scallions, ginger, mushrooms and corn for 1 minute. Add the spiced fish and cook for 2 minutes, turning once.

3 Mix together the soy sauce, sherry and sugar, then pour over the fish. Simmer for 2 minutes. Season to taste. Serve with noodles and stir-fried vegetables.

COOK'S TIP

Chinese noodles are available in most large supermarkets and make a very speedy accompaniment, since they only need to be soaked in boiling water for a few minutes before being drained and served.

FISH BALLS IN TOMATO SAUCE

This quick meal is a good choice for young children, as you can be sure there are no bones.

Preparation time 4 minutes
Cooking time 14 minutes

SERVES 4

1 pound white fish fillets, such as
*   haddock or cod, skinned*
4 tablespoons fresh whole-wheat
*   bread crumbs*
2 tablespoons snipped fresh chives
14-ounce can chopped tomatoes
½ cup button mushrooms, sliced
salt and ground black pepper

1 Cut the fish fillets into large chunks and place in a food processor. Add the whole-wheat bread crumbs and chives. Season to taste with salt and pepper, and process until the fish is finely chopped but still has some texture.

2 Divide the fish mixture into about 16 even-size pieces, then mold them into balls.

3 Place the tomatoes and mushrooms in a wide saucepan and cook over medium heat until boiling. Add the fish balls, cover and simmer for about 10 minutes, until cooked. Serve hot.

COOK'S TIPS

Instead of using a can of chopped tomatoes and fresh mushrooms, you could substitute a jar of ready-made tomato and mushroom sauce. Just add the fish balls and simmer for about 10 minutes. When making this dish for young children, try cooking the fish balls in their favorite canned tomato soup—even children who normally turn up their noses at anything other than fish sticks will love it.

MACKEREL KEBABS WITH PARSLEY DRESSING

Oily fish, such as mackerel, are ideal for broiling. They cook quickly and need no extra oil.

Preparation time 8 minutes
Cooking time 4 minutes

SERVES 4
1 pound mackerel fillets
finely grated zest and juice of
*   1 lemon*
3 tablespoons chopped fresh parsley
16 cherry tomatoes
8 pitted black olives
salt and ground black pepper

1 Cut the fish into 1½-inch chunks and toss in a bowl with half the lemon zest and juice, half the parsley and some seasoning.

2 Preheat the broiler. Thread the chunks of fish onto eight long wooden or metal skewers, alternating them with the cherry tomatoes and olives. Broil the kebabs for 3–4 minutes, turning the kebabs occasionally, until the fish is cooked.

3 Mix the remaining lemon zest and juice with the remaining parsley in a small bowl, then season to taste with salt and pepper. Spoon this dressing over the kebabs and serve hot, with plain boiled rice or noodles and a leafy green salad.

COOK'S TIP
When using wooden or bamboo kebab skewers, soak them in a bowl of cold water for 10 minutes to help prevent them from scorching.

VARIATIONS
Other firm-fleshed fish could be used in place of the mackerel—for a special occasion you could opt for salmon fillet or monkfish tail. Or try a mixture of the two, threading the fish chunks alternately onto the skewers with the tomatoes and olives.

SEAFOOD PILAF

This all-in-one-pan main course is a satisfying and surprisingly quick and easy meal for any day of the week. For a special meal, substitute dry white wine for the orange juice.

Preparation time 3 minutes
Cooking time 17 minutes

SERVES 4
2 teaspoons olive oil
1¼ cups long-grain rice
1 teaspoon ground turmeric
1 red bell pepper, seeded and diced
1 small onion, finely chopped
2 zucchini, sliced
1¼ cups button mushrooms, halved
1½ cups fish or chicken stock
⅔ cup orange juice
12 ounces white fish fillets, skinned and cubed
12 cooked, shelled mussels
salt and ground black pepper
grated zest of 1 orange, to garnish

1 Heat the oil in a large pan. Sauté the rice and ground turmeric over low heat for about 1 minute.

2 Add the pepper, onion, zucchini and mushrooms. Stir in the stock and orange juice. Bring to a boil.

3 Reduce the heat and add the fish. Cover and simmer gently for about 15 minutes, until the rice is tender and the liquid absorbed. Stir in the mussels and heat thoroughly. Adjust the seasoning, sprinkle with orange zest, and serve hot.

COOK'S TIP
If you prefer, use fresh mussels in the shell. Scrub well and discard any that remain open when tapped. Add to the pan 5 minutes before the end of cooking. Throw away any mussels that have not opened after cooking.

SALMON PASTA WITH PARSLEY SAUCE

Preparation time 5 minutes
Cooking time 10–12 minutes

SERVES 4
1 pound salmon fillet, skinned
2 cups dried pasta, such as penne or twists
6 ounces cherry tomatoes, halved
⅔ cup low-fat crème fraîche
3 tablespoons chopped fresh parsley
finely grated zest of ½ orange
salt and ground black pepper

COOK'S TIP
If you can't find low-fat crème fraîche, use ordinary crème fraîche or heavy cream instead.

1 Cut the salmon into bite-size pieces, arrange on a heatproof plate, and cover with foil.

2 Bring a large pan of salted water to a boil and add the pasta. Place the plate of salmon on top and cook for 10–12 minutes, until the pasta and salmon are cooked.

3 Drain the pasta and toss with the tomatoes and salmon. Mix together the crème fraîche, parsley, orange zest and pepper to taste, then toss with the salmon and pasta and serve hot or cold.

WARM SALMON SALAD

Light and fresh, this salad should be served immediately, or you'll find the salad greens will lose their bright color and texture.

Preparation time 4–5 minutes
Cooking time 7 minutes

SERVES 4

1 pound salmon fillet, skinned
2 tablespoons sesame oil
grated zest of ½ orange
juice of 1 orange
1 teaspoon Dijon mustard
1 tablespoon chopped fresh tarragon
3 tablespoons peanut oil
4 ounces haricots vert, trimmed
6 ounces mixed salad greens, such as
 young spinach leaves, radicchio,
 frisée and oakleaf lettuce leaves
1 tablespoon toasted sesame seeds

1 Cut the salmon into bite-size pieces, then make the dressing. Mix together the sesame oil, orange zest and juice, mustard, chopped tarragon and seasoning in a bowl.

2 Heat the peanut oil in a frying pan. Add the salmon pieces and fry for 3–4 minutes, until lightly browned but tender inside.

3 While the salmon is cooking, blanch the green beans in boiling salted water for 5–6 minutes, until crisp-tender.

4 Add the dressing to the salmon. Toss gently over the heat for 30 seconds. Remove from the heat.

5 Arrange the salad greens on serving plates. Drain the beans and arrange on top. Spoon the salmon and cooking juices on top and serve, sprinkled with the sesame seeds.

SALMON WITH WATERCRESS SAUCE

Preparation time 2–3 minutes
Cooking time 16 minutes

SERVES 4
1¼ cups crème fraîche
2 tablespoons chopped fresh tarragon
2 tablespoons unsalted butter
1 tablespoon sunflower oil
4 salmon fillets, skinned
1 garlic clove, crushed
½ cup dry white wine
1 bunch watercress
salt and ground black pepper

1   Gently heat the crème fraîche in a small pan until just beginning to boil. Remove the pan from the heat and stir in half the tarragon. Leave the herb cream to infuse while you cook the fish.

2   Heat the butter and oil in a frying pan, add the salmon and sauté for 3–5 minutes on each side. Remove from the pan; keep hot.

3   Add the garlic; sauté briefly, then add the wine and cook until reduced to 1 tablespoon.

4   Meanwhile, strip the leaves off the watercress stalks and chop finely. Discard any damaged leaves.

5   Strain the herb cream into the pan and cook for a few minutes, stirring until the sauce has thickened. Stir in the remaining tarragon and the watercress. Cook for a few minutes. Season, spoon over the salmon and serve.

SPANISH-STYLE HAKE

Cod and haddock steaks or cutlets will work just as well as hake.

Preparation time 3 minutes
Cooking time 15–16 minutes

SERVES 4
2 tablespoons olive oil
2 tablespoons butter
1 onion, chopped
3 garlic cloves, crushed
1 tablespoon all-purpose flour
½ teaspoon paprika
4 hake cutlets, about 6 ounces each
8 ounces green beans, chopped
1½ cups fish stock
⅔ cup dry white wine
2 tablespoons dry sherry
16–20 live mussels, cleaned
3 tablespoons chopped fresh parsley
salt and ground black pepper
crusty bread, to serve

1. Heat the oil and butter in a sauté or frying pan, add the onion and cook for 5 minutes, until softened, but not browned. Add the garlic and cook for 1 minute more.

2. Mix together the flour and paprika, then lightly dust over the hake cutlets. Push the onion and garlic to one side of the pan.

3. Add the hake cutlets to the pan and sauté until golden on both sides. Stir in the beans, stock, wine, sherry and seasoning. Bring to a boil and cook for about 2 minutes.

4. Add the mussels and parsley, cover the pan and cook until the mussels have opened.

5. Discard any mussels that have not opened, then serve the hake in warmed soup bowls with crusty bread to mop up the juices.

SPAGHETTI WITH SEAFOOD SAUCE

Preparation time 4 minutes
Cooking time 16 minutes

SERVES 4

3 tablespoons olive oil
1 medium onion, chopped
1 garlic clove, finely chopped
8 ounces spaghetti
2¹/₂ cups passata or tomato sauce
1 tablespoon tomato paste
1 teaspoon dried oregano
1 bay leaf
1 teaspoon sugar
2 cups cooked, peeled shrimp (rinsed
*   well if canned)*
1¹/₂ cups cooked clam or
*   cockle meat (rinsed well if canned)*
1 tablespoon lemon juice
3 tablespoons chopped fresh parsley
2 tablespoons butter
salt and ground black pepper
4 whole cooked shrimp, to garnish

[1] Heat the oil in a pan and add
the onion and garlic. Sauté over
moderate heat for 5 minutes, until the
onion has softened.

[2] Meanwhile, cook the spaghetti
in a large pan of boiling salted
water for 10–12 minutes. Stir the
passata, tomato paste, oregano, bay
leaf and sugar into the onion mixture
and season well. Bring to a boil,
then lower the heat and simmer for
2–3 minutes.

[3] Add the shellfish, lemon juice
and half the parsley. Stir, cover
and cook for 6–7 minutes.

[4] Drain the spaghetti when it is
just tender and add the butter
to the pan. Return the drained
spaghetti to the pan and toss with the
butter until well coated. Season well.

[5] Divide the spaghetti among
four warmed plates and top
with the seafood sauce. Sprinkle with
the remaining chopped parsley,
garnish with the whole shrimp and
serve immediately.

PAN-FRIED SHRIMP IN THEIR SHELLS

Although expensive, this is a very quick and simple dish, ideal for an impromptu supper with friends. Serve with hot crusty Italian bread to scoop up the juices.

Preparation time 2–3 minutes
Cooking time 5–8 minutes

SERVES 4
¼ cup extra virgin olive oil
32 large raw shrimp, in their shells
4 garlic cloves, finely chopped
½ cup Italian dry white vermouth
3 tablespoons passata or tomato sauce
salt and ground black pepper
chopped fresh flat-leaf parsley,
  to garnish
crusty bread, to serve

1 Heat the olive oil in a large, heavy frying pan until just sizzling. Add the shrimp and toss over medium to high heat until their shells just begin to turn pink. Sprinkle the garlic over the shrimp in the pan and toss again, then add the vermouth and let it bubble, tossing the shrimp constantly so that they cook evenly and absorb the flavors of the garlic and vermouth.

2 Keeping the pan on the heat, add the passata, with salt and pepper to taste. Stir until the shrimp are thoroughly coated in the sauce. Serve at once, sprinkled with the parsley and accompanied by plenty of hot crusty bread.

BROILED RED MULLET WITH ROSEMARY

This recipe is very simple—the taste of grilled red mullet is so good in itself that it needs very little to bring out the flavor.

Preparation time 10 minutes
Cooking time 10 minutes

SERVES 4
4 red mullet, cleaned, about
  10 ounces each
4 garlic cloves, cut into thin slivers
5 tablespoons olive oil
2 tablespoons balsamic vinegar
2 teaspoons very finely chopped
  fresh rosemary
ground black pepper
coarse sea salt, to serve
fresh rosemary sprigs and lemon
  wedges, to garnish

1 Cut three diagonal slits in both sides of each fish. Push the garlic slivers into the slits. Place the fish in a single layer in a shallow dish. Whisk the oil, vinegar and rosemary in a bowl and add ground black pepper to taste.

VARIATION
Red mullet are extra delicious cooked on the grill. If possible, enclose them in a hinged grill so that they are easy to turn over.

2 Pour the vinaigrette mixture over the fish, cover with plastic wrap and set aside for 8 minutes, or longer if you can spare the time. Lift the fish out of the dish and put it on the rack of a broiler pan. Reserve the marinade for basting.

3 Broil the fish for 5 minutes on each side, turning once and brushing with the marinade. Serve hot, sprinkled with coarse sea salt and garnished with fresh rosemary sprigs and lemon wedges.

MACKEREL WITH MUSTARD AND LEMON

Mackerel must be really fresh to be enjoyed. Look for bright, firm-looking fish.

Preparation time 5 minutes
Cooking time 10–12 minutes

SERVES 4

4 fresh mackerel, about 10 ounces
  each, gutted and cleaned
6–8 ounces young spinach leaves
For the mustard and lemon butter
½ cup butter, melted
2 tablespoons whole-grain mustard
grated zest of 1 lemon
2 tablespoons lemon juice
3 tablespoons chopped fresh parsley
salt and ground black pepper

1 Cut off the mackerel heads just behind the gills, using a sharp knife, then slit the bellies so that each fish can be opened out flat.

2 Place the fish skin side up. With the heel of your hand, press along the backbone to loosen it.

3 Turn the fish the right way up and pull the bone away. Cut off the tail and cut each fish in half lengthwise. Wash and pat dry.

4 Score the skin three or four times, then season the fish. To make the mustard and lemon butter, mix together the melted butter, mustard, lemon zest and juice, parsley and seasoning. Place the mackerel on a broiler rack. Brush a little of the butter over the mackerel and broil for 5 minutes each side, basting occasionally, until cooked through.

5 Arrange the spinach leaves in the center of four large plates. Place the mackerel on top. Heat the remaining flavored butter in a small pan until sizzling and pour over the mackerel. Serve at once.

PAN-STEAMED MUSSELS WITH THAI HERBS

Another simple and speedy dish. The lemongrass adds a refreshing tang.

Preparation time 5 minutes
Cooking time 5–7 minutes

SERVES 4–6

2¼ pounds mussels, cleaned and
   beards removed
2 lemongrass stalks, finely chopped
4 shallots, chopped
4 kaffir lime leaves, roughly torn
2 red chiles, sliced
1 tablespoon fish sauce
2 tablespoons lime juice
chopped scallions and cilantro leaves,
   to garnish

1 Place all the ingredients except the scallions and cilantro in a large pan. Stir well.

2 Cover the pan and place it over medium-high heat. Steam for 5–7 minutes, shaking the saucepan occasionally, until the mussels open. Discard any mussels that do not open.

3 Lift out the cooked mussels with a slotted spoon and place on a serving dish.

4 Garnish the mussels with the chopped scallions and cilantro leaves. Serve immediately.

CHILE SHRIMP

This delightful, spicy combination makes a lovely light main course for a casual supper. Serve with rice, noodles or freshly cooked pasta and a leafy salad.

Preparation time 5 minutes
Cooking time 15 minutes

SERVES 3–4
3 tablespoons olive oil
2 shallots, chopped
2 garlic cloves, chopped
1 red chile, chopped
1 pound ripe tomatoes, peeled, seeded
    and chopped
1 tablespoon tomato paste
1 bay leaf
1 thyme sprig
6 tablespoons dry white wine
1 pound cooked, peeled large shrimp
salt and ground black pepper
roughly torn basil leaves, to garnish

1 Heat the oil in a pan, then add the shallots, garlic and chile. Sauté until the garlic starts to brown.

2 Add the tomatoes, tomato paste, bay leaf, thyme, wine and seasoning. Bring to a boil, then reduce the heat and cook gently for about 10 minutes, stirring occasionally, until the sauce has thickened. Discard the herbs.

3 Stir the shrimp into the sauce and heat through for a few minutes. Taste and adjust the seasoning. Sprinkle the basil leaves on top and serve at once.

COOK'S TIP
For a milder flavor, remove all the seeds from the chile.

SCALLOPS WITH GINGER

Scallops need little cooking, so they are ideal for spontaneous suppers.

Preparation time 6 minutes
Cooking time 6–7 minutes

SERVES 4
8–12 sea scallops
3 tablespoons butter
1-inch piece of fresh ginger,
    finely chopped
1 bunch scallions, diagonally sliced
¼ cup white vermouth
1 cup crème fraîche
salt and ground black pepper
chopped fresh parsley, to garnish

1 Remove the tough muscle opposite the coral on each scallop. Separate the coral and cut the white part of the scallop in half horizontally.

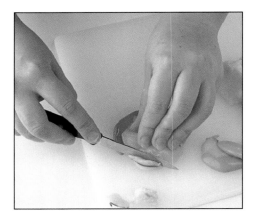

2 Melt the butter in a frying pan. Add the scallops, including the corals, and sauté for about 2 minutes, until lightly browned. Take care not to overcook the scallops, as this will toughen them. Lift out the scallops with a slotted spoon and transfer to a warmed serving dish. Keep hot.

3 Add the ginger and scallions to the pan and stir-fry for 2 minutes. Pour in the vermouth and allow to bubble until it has almost evaporated. Stir in the crème fraîche and cook for a few minutes, until thickened. Season.

4 Pour the sauce over the scallops, garnish and serve.

THAI SHRIMP SALAD

This salad has the marvelous aromatic flavor of lemongrass.

Preparation time 17 minutes
Cooking time None

SERVES 4

*9 ounces cooked, peeled extra-large
   tiger shrimp
1 tablespoon fish sauce
2 tablespoons lime juice
1½ teaspoons light brown sugar
1 small red chile, finely chopped
1 scallion, finely chopped
1 small garlic clove, crushed
1-inch piece of fresh lemongrass,
   finely chopped
2 tablespoons chopped cilantro
3 tablespoons dry white wine
8–12 romaine lettuce leaves, to serve
cilantro sprigs, to garnish*

1 Place the tiger shrimp in a bowl and add all the remaining ingredients except the lettuce. Stir well, cover and set aside for about 15 minutes, mixing and turning the shrimp occasionally.

2 Arrange two or three of the lettuce leaves on each of four individual serving plates.

3 Spoon the shrimp salad into the lettuce leaves. Garnish with cilantro and serve at once.

COOK'S TIP
If you obtain raw shrimp, cook them in boiling water until pink and use instead of the cooked shrimp.

CAJUN-SPICED FISH

Cajun food is becoming increasingly popular outside its native New Orleans, and no wonder, since dishes like this one cook quickly and taste absolutely superb.

Preparation time 2–3 minutes
Cooking time 10–13 minutes

SERVES 4

*1 teaspoon dried thyme
1 teaspoon dried oregano
1 teaspoon ground black pepper
¼ teaspoon cayenne pepper
2 teaspoons paprika
½ teaspoon garlic salt
4 tail-end pieces of cod fillet
   (about 6 ounces each)
6 tablespoons butter
½ red bell pepper, seeded and sliced
½ green bell pepper, seeded and sliced
fresh thyme, to garnish
grilled tomatoes and sweet potato
   purée, to serve (optional)*

1 Place all the herbs and spices in a bowl and mix well. Lightly coat the fish in the spice mixture.

2 Heat 2 tablespoons of the butter in a frying pan, add the peppers and sauté gently for 5 minutes. Remove the peppers and

3 Add the remaining butter to the pan and heat until sizzling. Add the cod fillets; sauté over moderate heat for 3–4 minutes on each side, until browned and cooked.

4 Transfer the fish to a warmed serving dish, surround with the peppers and garnish with thyme. Serve the spiced fish with some grilled tomatoes and sweet potato purée, if you like.

COOK'S TIP
This blend of herbs and spices can be used to flavor any fish steaks or fillets and could also be used to jazz up panfried shrimp.

QUICK PITA PIZZAS

Pita breads make very good crusts for quick thin and crispy pizzas, and they are easy to eat with your hands, too. The perfect speedy snack.

Preparation time 5 minutes
Cooking time 8–10 minutes

SERVES 4
4 pita breads
7-fluid-ounce jar pasta sauce
8 ounces mozzarella cheese, sliced
  or grated
dried oregano or thyme, to sprinkle
salt and ground black pepper
Extra toppings—choose from
1 small red onion, thinly sliced and
  lightly sautéed
3 ounces (¾ cup) button mushrooms,
  sliced and sautéed
7-ounce can corn, drained
2 jalapeño peppers, sliced
black or green olives, pitted
  and sliced
capers, drained

1 Prepare two or three toppings of your choice for the pizzas.

2 Preheat the broiler and lightly toast the pita breads on both sides until golden.

COOK'S TIP
Teenagers love pita pizzas, especially if they can assemble their own toppings. Strips of fried bacon and sliced pepperoni are great for nonvegetarians.

3 Spread pasta sauce on each pita, right to the edge. This prevents the edges of the pitas from burning when they are returned to the broiler.

4 Arrange cheese slices or grated cheese on top of each pita and sprinkle with dried oregano or thyme. Add salt and pepper to taste.

5 Add the toppings of your choice and then broil the pizzas for 5–8 minutes, until they are golden brown and bubbling. Serve the pita pizzas immediately.

FRENCH BREAD PIZZAS WITH ARTICHOKES

Crunchy French bread makes an ideal crust for these quick pizzas.

Preparation time 4 minutes
Cooking time 14–16 minutes

SERVES 4

1 tablespoon sunflower oil
1 onion, chopped
1 green bell pepper, seeded and chopped
7-ounce can chopped tomatoes
1 tablespoon tomato paste
½ French bread
14-ounce can or jar artichoke hearts,
   drained
4 ounces mozzarella cheese, sliced
1 tablespoon poppy seeds
salt and ground black pepper

1   Heat the oil in a frying pan. Add the chopped onion and pepper and cook for 4 minutes, until just softened.

2   Stir in the chopped tomatoes and the tomato paste. Cook for 4 minutes, stirring occasionally, then remove from the heat and add salt and pepper to taste.

3   Cut the piece of French bread in half lengthwise. Cut each half in four to give eight pieces in all.

4   Spoon a little of the pepper and tomato mixture over each piece of bread. Preheat the broiler.

5   Slice the artichoke hearts. Arrange them on top of the pepper and tomato mixture. Cover with the mozzarella slices and sprinkle with the poppy seeds.

6   Arrange the French bread pizzas on a rack over a broiler pan and broil for 6–8 minutes, until the cheese melts and is beginning to brown. Serve at once.

BRIOCHE WITH MIXED MUSHROOMS

Mushrooms, served on toasted brioche, make a delectable lunch.

Preparation time 3–4 minutes
Cooking time 15 minutes

SERVES 4
6 tablespoons butter
1 vegetable bouillon cube
1 pound (4 cups) shiitake
  mushrooms, caps only, sliced
8 ounces (2 cups) button mushrooms,
  sliced
3 tablespoons dry sherry
1 cup crème fraîche
2 teaspoons lemon juice
8 thick slices of brioche
salt and ground black pepper
fresh thyme, to garnish (optional)

1 Melt the butter in a large pan. Crumble in the bouillon cube and stir for about 30 seconds.

COOK'S TIP
If shiitake mushrooms are not available, substitute more button mushrooms.

2 Add the shiitake and button mushrooms to the pan and cook for 5 minutes over moderate to high heat, stirring occasionally.

3 Stir in the dry sherry. Cook for 1 minute, then add the crème fraîche. Cook, stirring, over gentle heat for 5 minutes. Stir in the lemon juice and add salt and pepper to taste. Preheat the broiler.

4 Toast the brioche slices under the broiler until just golden on both sides. Spoon the mushrooms on top, run briefly under the broiler, and serve. Fresh thyme can be used to garnish, if you like.

MIXED PEPPER PIPERADE

Preparation time 3–4 minutes
Cooking time 15 minutes

SERVES 4
2 tablespoons olive oil
1 onion, chopped
1 red bell pepper
1 green bell pepper
4 tomatoes, peeled and chopped
1 garlic clove, crushed
4 large eggs
ground black pepper
whole-wheat toast, to serve

1   Heat the oil in a large frying pan and sauté the onion gently until it becomes softened.

2   Remove the seeds from the peppers and slice them thinly. Stir the pepper slices into the onion and cook together gently for 5 minutes. Add the tomatoes and garlic, season with black pepper, and cook for another 5 minutes, or until the mixture has thickened slightly.
In a small bowl or measuring cup, beat the eggs with 1 tablespoon water.

3   Pour the egg mixture over the vegetables in the frying pan and cook for 2–3 minutes, stirring now and then, until the pipérade has thickened to the consistency of lightly scrambled eggs. Serve immediately with hot whole-wheat toast.

COOK'S TIPS
Choose eggs that have been date-stamped for freshness. Do not stir the pipérade too much, or the eggs may become rubbery.

BROCCOLI AND CAULIFLOWER GRATIN

Broccoli and cauliflower make an attractive combination; this dish has a simple sauce based on yogurt.

Preparation time 3 minutes
Cooking time 11 minutes

SERVES 4
1 small cauliflower, about 9 ounces
1 small head broccoli, about 9 ounces
²/₃ cup plain yogurt
1 cup grated Cheddar or Red Leicester
  cheese
1 teaspoon wholegrain mustard
2 tablespoons whole-wheat bread
  crumbs
salt and ground black pepper

1 Break the cauliflower and broccoli into small florets, then cook in boiling salted water for about 8 minutes, or until tender. Drain thoroughly, then transfer to a flameproof dish.

2 Mix the yogurt, cheese and mustard. Season with pepper and spoon over the cauliflower and broccoli. Preheat the broiler.

3 Sprinkle the bread crumbs over the top of the sauced vegetables and place under the hot broiler until golden brown. Serve at once.

COOK'S TIP

When preparing the cauliflower and broccoli, discard the tougher part of the stalk, then break the florets into same-size pieces, so that they cook evenly. Any tender pieces of stalk on the broccoli can be peeled, thinly sliced and cooked with the florets.

CRACKED WHEAT AND FENNEL SALAD

Preparation time 18 minutes
Cooking time 2 minutes

SERVES 4
¾ cup cracked wheat
4 ounces green beans, chopped
1 large fennel bulb, finely chopped
1 small orange, zest grated
1 garlic clove, crushed
2–3 tablespoons sunflower oil
1 tablespoon white wine vinegar
salt and ground black pepper
chopped red or orange pepper,
  to garnish

1 Place the cracked wheat in a bowl and cover with boiling water. Let sit for 10 minutes. Drain well and squeeze out any excess water. Pour into a bowl.

2 Blanch the green beans in boiling water for 2 minutes. Drain. Stir into the drained wheat with the fennel. Peel and segment the orange and stir into the salad.

3 Add the garlic to the orange zest, then add the oil, wine vinegar and seasoning to taste, and mix thoroughly. Pour the dressing over the salad and mix well. If time permits, chill the salad for 1–2 hours.

4 Serve the salad sprinkled with the red or orange pepper.

RUNNER BEANS WITH TOMATOES

Young runner beans should not have "strings" down the sides, but older ones will, and the strings should be removed before cooking.

Preparation time 2 minutes
Cooking time 13–18 minutes

SERVES 4
1½ pounds runner beans, sliced
3 tablespoons butter
4 ripe tomatoes, peeled and chopped
salt and ground black pepper
chopped fresh tarragon, to garnish

COOK'S TIP
Green beans can be used instead of runner beans, but reduce the cooking time slightly.

1 Add the beans to a saucepan of boiling water, return to a boil, then boil for 3 minutes. Drain well.

2 Heat the butter in a saucepan and add the tomatoes, beans and seasoning. Cover the pan and simmer gently for 10–15 minutes, until the beans are tender.

3 Place the beans and tomatoes in a warm serving dish and sprinkle the chopped tarragon over them. Serve hot as an accompaniment.

SPINACH AND BEET SALAD

Preparation time 5 minutes
Cooking time 1 minute

SERVES 4–6
7 ounces young spinach leaves
3 tablespoons light olive oil
1 teaspoon caraway seeds
juice of 1 orange
1 teaspoon sugar
1½ pounds cooked beets, diced
salt and ground black pepper
chopped fresh parsley, to garnish

1 Arrange the spinach leaves in a shallow salad bowl.

2 Heat the oil in a saucepan. Add the caraway seeds, orange juice and sugar. Shake over the heat to warm through.

3 Add the beets and shake the pan to coat with the dressing.

4 Spoon the warm beet and dressing mixture over the spinach leaves and sprinkle with the chopped parsley. Serve at once either as an accompaniment or as a main course.

COOK'S TIP
Use freshly cooked beets, not those that have been steeped in vinegar.

VEGETABLE AND SATAY SALAD

To make this tasty salad in the allotted time, you will need to cook the potatoes and the other vegetables simultaneously.

Preparation time 5 minutes
Cooking time 12–14 minutes

SERVES 4
1 pound baby new potatoes
1 small head cauliflower, broken into small florets
8 ounces green beans, trimmed
14-ounce can chickpeas, drained
2 cups watercress sprigs
2 cups bean sprouts
8 scallions, sliced
4 tablespoons crunchy peanut butter
²/₃ cup hot water
1 teaspoon chili sauce
2 teaspoons brown sugar
1 teaspoon soy sauce
1 teaspoon lime juice

1   Put the potatoes in a pan and add water just to cover. Bring to a boil and cook for 10–12 minutes, or until the potatoes are just tender when pierced with the point of a sharp knife. Drain and refresh under cold running water. Drain the potatoes again.

2   Meanwhile, bring another pan of salted water to a boil. Add the cauliflower and cook for about 5 minutes, then add the beans and cook for 5 minutes more. Drain both vegetables, refresh under cold water and drain again.

3   Put the cauliflower and beans in a large bowl and add the chickpeas. Halve the potatoes and add. Toss lightly. Mix the watercress, bean sprouts and scallions. Divide among four plates and pile the cooked vegetables on top.

4   Put the peanut butter in a bowl and stir in the water. Add the chili sauce, brown sugar, soy sauce and lime juice. Whisk well, then drizzle the dressing over the salad. Serve at once, with lime wedges if you like.

ZUCCHINI PUFFS WITH MIXED GREEN SALAD

This unusual salad consists of deep-fried zucchini, flavored with mint and served warm on a bed of salad greens with a balsamic dressing.

Preparation time 5 minutes
Cooking time 6 minutes

SERVES 2–3
1 pound zucchini
1½ cups fresh white bread crumbs
1 egg
pinch of cayenne pepper
1 tablespoon chopped fresh mint
oil for deep frying
1 tablespoon balsamic vinegar
3 tablespoons extra virgin olive oil
7 ounces mixed salad greens
salt and ground black pepper

1 Trim the zucchini. Coarsely grate them and put in a colander. Squeeze out the excess water, then put the zucchini in a bowl.

2 Add the bread crumbs, egg, cayenne pepper and chopped fresh mint, with salt and pepper to taste. Mix well, with a spoon or clean hands.

3 Shape the zucchini and bread crumb mixture into balls about the size of walnuts.

4 Heat the oil for deep-frying to 350°F, or until a cube of bread, when added to the oil, browns in 30–40 seconds. Deep-fry the zucchini balls in batches for 2 minutes. Drain on paper towels.

5 Whisk the vinegar and oil together and season well.

6 Put the salad greens in a bowl and pour the dressing over them. Toss lightly to coat the greens evenly. Add the zucchini puffs and toss lightly together. Serve at once, while the zucchini puffs are still crisp.

Herb Omelet with Tomato Salad

This is ideal as a snack or a light lunch—use flavorful, fresh plum tomatoes in season.

Preparation time 6 minutes
Cooking time 6 minutes

SERVES 4
4 eggs, beaten
2 tablespoons chopped, mixed fresh herbs
pat of butter
3–4 tablespoons olive oil
1 tablespoon fresh orange juice
1 teaspoon red wine vinegar
1 teaspoon grainy mustard
2 large tomatoes, thinly sliced
salt and ground black pepper
fresh herb sprigs, to garnish

1 Beat the eggs, herbs and seasoning together. Heat the butter and a little of the oil in an omelet pan.

2 When the fats are just sizzling, pour in the egg mixture and allow to set for about 5 minutes, until almost cooked through, stirring very occasionally with a fork.

3 Meanwhile, heat the rest of the oil in a small pan with the orange juice, vinegar and mustard, and add salt and pepper to taste.

4 Roll up the cooked omelet and cut neatly into ¹/₂-inch-wide strips. Keep them rolled up and transfer immediately to warmed plates.

5 Arrange the sliced tomatoes on the plates with the omelet rolls and pour the warm dressing on top. Garnish with herb sprigs and serve.

Three-cheese Croutes

Preparation time 2–3 minutes
Cooking time 10–15 minutes

SERVES 2–4
4 thick slices of slightly stale bread
a little butter or mustard
3 ounces Brie cheese
3 tablespoons fromage frais
¹/₂ cup grated Parmesan or mature Cheddar cheese
1 small garlic clove, crushed
salt and ground black pepper
black olives, to garnish

COOK'S TIPS
If you have Brie that will not ripen fully, this is an excellent way of using it up. You'll need a knife and fork to eat this tasty appetizer. Instead of the simple black olive garnish, you could serve it with tangy whole-fruit cranberry sauce.

1 Preheat the oven to 400°F. Place the bread slices on a baking sheet and spread with either butter or mustard.

2 Cut the Brie into thin slices and arrange evenly on the bread.

3 Mix together the fromage frais, Parmesan or Cheddar, garlic and seasoning to taste. Spread over the Brie and bread, taking the mixture right to the corners.

4 Bake for 10–15 minutes, or until golden and bubbling. Serve immediately, garnished with black olives.

LEMON AND PARMESAN CAPELLINI WITH HERB BREAD

Cream is thickened with Parmesan and flavored with lemon to make a superb sauce for pasta.

Preparation time 5 minutes
Cooking time 2–12 minutes

SERVES 2
½ whole-wheat baguette
4 tablespoons butter, softened
1 garlic clove, crushed
2 tablespoons chopped fresh herbs
8 ounces dried or fresh capellini
1 cup light cream
3 ounces Parmesan cheese, grated
finely grated zest of 1 lemon
salt and ground black pepper

1   Preheat the oven to 400°F. Cut the baguette into thick slices.

2   Put the butter in a bowl and beat with the garlic and herbs. Spread thickly over each slice of bread.

3   Reassemble the baguette. The garlic herb butter will help to hold the slices together. Wrap in foil, set on a baking sheet and bake for 10 minutes.

4   Meanwhile, bring a large pan of water to a boil and cook the pasta until just tender. Dried pasta will take 10–12 minutes; fresh pasta will be ready in 2–3 minutes.

5   Pour the cream into another pan and bring to a boil. Stir in the Parmesan and lemon zest. The sauce should thicken in 30 seconds or so.

6   Drain the pasta, return it to the pan and toss with the sauce. Season to taste and sprinkle with a little chopped fresh parsley and more grated lemon zest, if you like. Serve with the hot herb bread.

TAGLIATELLE WITH TOMATOES AND BLACK OLIVES

Sun-dried tomatoes add pungency to this dish, while the grilled fresh tomatoes give it a bit of bite.

Preparation time 5 minutes
Cooking time 10–12 minutes

SERVES 4

3 tablespoons olive oil
1 garlic clove, crushed
1 small onion, chopped
4 tablespoons dry white wine
6 sun-dried tomatoes, chopped
2 tablespoons chopped fresh parsley
1/2 cup pitted black olives, halved
1 pound fresh tagliatelle
4 tomatoes, halved
Parmesan cheese, to serve
salt and ground black pepper

1   Heat 2 tablespoons of the oil in a pan. Add the garlic and onion and cook for 2–3 minutes, stirring occasionally. Add the wine, sun-dried tomatoes and the parsley. Cook for 2 minutes. Stir in the black olives, lower the heat and leave the sauce over low heat.

COOK'S TIP

It is essential to buy Parmesan in a piece for this dish. Find a good source—fresh Parmesan should not be unacceptably hard—and shave or grate it yourself. The flavor will be much more intense than that of the grated product.

2   Preheat the broiler. Bring a large pan of salted water to a boil. Add the fresh tagliatelle and cook for 2–3 minutes.

3   Put the tomatoes on a baking sheet and brush with the remaining oil. Broil for 3–4 minutes.

4   When the pasta rises to the surface of the boiling water, it is ready. Drain it thoroughly, return it to the pan and toss with the sauce. Pile into a bowl and add the grilled tomatoes. Grind black pepper over the top and add Parmesan shavings.

PASTA WITH BROCCOLI AND ARTICHOKES

Preparation time 5 minutes

Cooking time 13 minutes

Serves 4

7 tablespoons olive oil

1 red bell pepper, quartered, seeded, and thinly sliced

1 onion, halved and thinly sliced

1 teaspoon dried thyme

3 tablespoons sherry vinegar

1 pound fresh or dried pasta shapes, such as penne or fusilli

2 x 6-ounce jars marinated artichoke hearts, drained and thinly sliced

1 cup cooked broccoli, chopped

20–25 black olives, pitted and chopped

2 tablespoons chopped fresh parsley

salt and ground black pepper

1 Heat 2 tablespoons of the oil in a nonstick frying pan. Add the pepper and onion and cook over low heat for 8–10 minutes, or until the vegetables are just soft, stirring occasionally.

2 Stir in the thyme and sherry vinegar. Cook for 30 seconds more, stirring, then set aside.

3 Meanwhile, cook the pasta in a large pan of boiling salted water until just tender (10–12 minutes for dried; 2–3 minutes for fresh). Drain, then transfer to a serving large bowl. Add 2 tablespoons of the oil and toss well to coat.

4 Add the artichokes, broccoli, olives, parsley, onion mixture and remaining oil to the pasta. Season with salt and pepper. Toss to blend. Let stand for 5 minutes before serving, longer if time permits.

PASTA WITH SPRING VEGETABLES

Preparation and
cooking time 20 minutes

SERVES 4

1 cup broccoli florets
4 ounces baby leeks
8 ounces asparagus, trimmed
1 small fennel bulb
2 cups fresh or frozen peas
3 tablespoons butter
1 shallot, chopped
3 tablespoons chopped mixed herbs,
   such as parsley, thyme and sage
1¼ cups heavy cream
12 ounces dried penne pasta
salt and ground black pepper
freshly grated Parmesan cheese,
   to serve

1 Divide the broccoli florets into
tiny sprigs. Cut the leeks and
asparagus diagonally into 2-inch
lengths. Trim the fennel bulb and cut
into wedges.

2 Cook the vegetables in boiling
salted water until just tender.
Remove with a slotted spoon and
keep hot.

3 Melt the butter in a separate
pan, add the chopped shallot
and cook, stirring occasionally, until
softened but not browned. Stir in the
herbs and cream and cook for a few
minutes, until slightly thickened.

4 Meanwhile, cook the pasta in
boiling salted water until just
tender. Drain well and add to the
sauce with the vegetables. Toss
gently and season with black pepper.

5 Serve the pasta at once with a
generous sprinkling of freshly
grated Parmesan.

RED FRIED RICE

*This vibrant rice dish owes
its appeal as much to the bright
colors of red onion, red pepper and
cherry tomatoes as it does to their
distinctive flavors.*

Preparation time 3–4 minutes
Cooking time 13–15 minutes

SERVES 2

*1 cup basmati rice
2 tablespoons peanut oil
1 large red onion, chopped
1 red bell pepper, seeded and chopped
12 ounces cherry tomatoes, halved
4 eggs, beaten
salt and ground black pepper*

1   Wash the rice several times in a bowl of cold water. Drain well. Bring a large pan of water to a boil, add the rice and cook for 10–12 minutes.

2   Meanwhile, heat the oil in a wok until very hot. Add the onion and pepper and stir-fry for 2–3 minutes. Add the cherry tomatoes and stir-fry for another 2 minutes.

3   Pour in the beaten eggs all at once. Cook for 30 seconds without stirring, then stir to break up the egg as it sets.

4   Drain the cooked rice thoroughly, add to the wok and toss it over the heat with the egg and vegetable mixture for 3 minutes. Season to taste.

KEDGEREE WITH GREEN BEANS AND MUSHROOMS

Crunchy cooked green beans and cremini mushrooms are the star ingredients in this vegetarian version of an old favorite.

Preparation time 3–4 minutes
Cooking time 16 minutes

SERVES 2–3
scant ¾ cup basmati rice
3 eggs
6 ounces green beans, trimmed
4 tablespoons butter
1 onion, finely chopped
2 cups cremini mushrooms, quartered
2 tablespoons light cream
1 tablespoon chopped fresh parsley
salt and ground black pepper

1 Wash the rice several times in a bowl of cold water. Drain thoroughly. Bring a pan of water to a boil, add the rice and cook for 10–12 minutes, until the grains are just tender.

2 Meanwhile, half-fill a second pan with water, add the eggs and bring to a boil. Lower the heat and simmer for 8 minutes. Drain the eggs, cool them under cold water, then remove the shells.

3 Bring another pan of water to a boil and cook the green beans for 5 minutes. Drain, refresh under cold running water, then drain again.

4 Melt the butter in a large frying pan. Add the onion and mushrooms. Cook for 2–3 minutes over moderate heat.

VARIATION
Leave out the beans and cook two sliced celery ribs with the onion and mushrooms. Garnish with toasted almonds.

5 Drain the rice well and add it to the onion mixture with the beans. Stir lightly. Cook for about 2 minutes. Cut the hard-boiled eggs into wedges and add them to the pan.

6 Stir in the cream and parsley, taking care not to break up the eggs. Reheat the kedgeree, but do not allow it to boil. Serve at once.

RED FRUIT PHYLLO BASKETS

Phyllo pastry is light as air and makes a very elegant dessert.

Preparation time 8 minutes
Cooking time 6–8 minutes

SERVES 6
3 sheets phyllo pastry (about 3½ ounces)
1 tablespoon sunflower oil
1½ cups soft fruits, such as red currants, strawberries and raspberries
1 cup strained plain yogurt
1 teaspoon confectioners' sugar

1 Preheat the oven to 400°F. Cut the sheets of phyllo pastry into 18 squares with sides about 4 inches long. Cover the phyllo with plastic wrap to prevent it from drying out.

2 Brush each phyllo square very thinly with oil, and then arrange the squares overlapping in six cups of a muffin pan, layering them in threes. Bake for 6–8 minutes, until crisp and golden. Lift the baskets out carefully and let them cool for 5–10 minutes on a wire rack.

3 Reserve a few sprigs of red currants on their stems for decoration and remove the rest from the stems. Stir into the yogurt with the strawberries and raspberries.

4 Spoon the yogurt mixture into the phyllo baskets. Decorate them with the reserved sprigs of red currants and sprinkle them with confectioners' sugar to serve.

VARIATIONS
Other soft fruits can be used instead of red currants, strawberries and raspberries. Try blueberries or blackberries for a change, or use sliced bananas, nectarines, peaches or kiwifruit.

APPLE SOUFFLE OMELETTE

Apples sautéed until they are soft and slightly caramelized make a delicious autumn filling.

Preparation time 3–4 minutes
Cooking time 8 minutes

SERVES 2

4 eggs, separated
2 tablespoons light cream
1 tablespoon sugar
1 tablespoon butter
confectioners' sugar, for dredging
For the filling
1 eating apple, peeled, cored
  and sliced
2 tablespoons butter
2 tablespoons light brown sugar
3 tablespoons light cream

1 To make the filling, sauté the apple slices in the butter and sugar until just tender. Stir in the cream and keep warm.

2 Beat the egg yolks with the cream and sugar. Beat the egg whites until stiff, then fold into the yolk mixture. Preheat the broiler.

3 Melt the butter in a large heavy frying pan, pour in the soufflé mixture and spread evenly. Cook until golden underneath, then brown the top under the broiler.

4 Slide the omelet onto a plate, add the apple mixture, then fold over. Sift the confectioners' sugar over thickly, then mark with a hot metal skewer. Serve immediately.

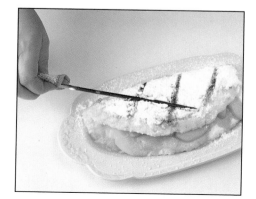

PINEAPPLE FLAMBE

Flambéing means adding alcohol and then burning it off so the flavor is not too overpowering.

Preparation time 5 minutes
Cooking time 1–2 minutes

SERVES 4
1 large, ripe pineapple
3 tablespoons unsalted butter
3 tablespoons light brown sugar
4 tablespoons fresh orange juice
2 tablespoons brandy
2 tablespoons sliced almonds, toasted

2 Cut the pineapple into thin slices and, with an apple corer, remove the hard central core.

1 Cut away the top and bottom of the pineapple. Then cut down the sides, removing all the dark "eyes," but leaving the pineapple in a good shape.

3 In a large frying pan, melt the butter with the sugar and orange juice. Add the pineapple slices and cook for about a minute, turning the slices once.

4 Add the brandy and light with a match immediately. Let the flames die down and then sprinkle with the almonds and serve with ice cream or thick, creamy yogurt.

WARM PEARS IN CIDER

Preparation and
cooking time 20 minutes

SERVES 4
1 lemon
¼ cup sugar
a little grated nutmeg
1 cup sweet cider
4 firm, ripe pears

1 Carefully remove the zest from the lemon with a potato peeler, leaving any white pith behind.

2 Squeeze the juice from the lemon into a saucepan, add the zest, sugar, nutmeg and cider and heat through to dissolve the sugar.

3 Carefully peel the pears, leaving the stems on if possible, and place them in the pan of sweetened, spiced cider. Poach the pears over medium heat for 10–15 minutes, until almost tender, turning them frequently.

4 Transfer the pears to individual serving dishes using a slotted spoon. Simmer the liquid over high heat until it reduces slightly and becomes syrupy.

5 Pour the warm syrup over the pears, and serve at once with freshly made custard, whipped cream or ice cream.

COOK'S TIP
To get pears of just the right firmness, you may have to buy them slightly underripe and then wait a day or more. Soft pears are no good at all for this dish.

COOL GREEN FRUIT SALAD

A sophisticated, simple fruit salad for any time of year.

Preparation time 20 minutes
Cooking time 30 seconds

SERVES 6
3 Ogen or Galia melons
1 cup green seedless grapes
2 kiwifruit
1 star fruit
1 green-skinned apple
1 lime
³⁄₄ cup sparkling white grape juice

1 Cut the melons in half and scoop out the seeds. Keeping the shells intact, scoop out the flesh with a melon baller, or scoop it out with a spoon and cut into bite-size cubes. Reserve the melon shells.

2 Remove any stems from the grapes, and, if they are large, cut them in half. Peel and chop the kiwifruit. Thinly slice the star fruit. Core and thinly slice the apple and place the slices in a bowl, with the melon, grapes, kiwifruit and star fruit. Mix gently.

3 Thinly pare the zest from the lime and cut it into fine strips. Blanch the strips in boiling water for 30 seconds, and then drain them and rinse them in cold water. Squeeze the juice from the lime and toss it with the fruit.

4 Spoon the prepared fruit into the reserved melon shells. Chill the shells if you have time, or serve at once, spooning the sparkling grape juice over the fruit and sprinkling the lime zest over it.

COOK'S TIP
If you're serving this dessert on a hot summer day, serve the filled melon shells nestled on a platter of crushed ice to keep them beautifully cool.

PRUNE AND ORANGE POTS

A simple, pantry dessert, made in minutes. It can be served right away, but is best chilled for about half an hour before serving.

Preparation time 4 minutes
Cooking time 7 minutes

SERVES 4
1 cup prunes
²⁄₃ cup fresh orange juice
1 cup plain yogurt
thin shreds of orange zest,
   to decorate

VARIATIONS

This dessert can also be made with other dried fruit, such as apricots or peaches. For a special occasion, add a dash of brandy or Cointreau with the yogurt.

1   Remove the pits from the prunes and roughly chop them. Place them in a pan and pour in the orange juice.

3   Remove from the heat, allow to cool slightly and then beat well with a wooden spoon, until the fruit breaks down to a rough purée.

5   Spoon the mixture into four bowls or stemmed glasses. Smooth the tops, but don't lose the swirled effect.

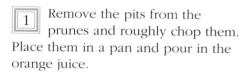

2   Bring the juice to a boil, stirring. Reduce the heat, cover and let simmer for 5 minutes, until the prunes are tender and the liquid is reduced by half.

4   Transfer the mixture to a bowl. Stir in the yogurt, swirling the yogurt and fruit purée together lightly with a spoon, to give an attractive marbled effect.

6   Blanch the shreds of orange zest in boiling water, drain and use a few shreds to decorate each dessert. Serve at once or chill if time permits.

ORANGE YOGURT BRULEE

A luxurious treat, but one that is much lower in fat than the classic crème brûlée, which is made with cream, eggs and large amounts of sugar.

Preparation time 6–8 minutes
Cooking time 3–4 minutes

SERVES 4
2 oranges
⅔ cup strained plain yogurt
4 tablespoons crème fraîche
3 tablespoons turbinado sugar
2 tablespoons light brown sugar

[1] With a sharp knife, cut away all the peel and white pith from the oranges and chop the fruit. Or, if there's time, segment the oranges, removing all the membrane.

[2] Place the fruit in the bottom of four individual flameproof dishes. Mix together the yogurt and crème fraîche and spoon the mixture over the oranges. Preheat the broiler.

[3] Mix together the two sugars and sprinkle them thickly and evenly over the tops of the dishes.

[4] Place the dishes under the broiler, close to the heat, for 3–4 minutes, or until the sugar melts and turns a rich golden brown. Serve warm or cold.

COOK'S TIP
For a lighter version, simply use 1 cup low-fat plain yogurt instead of the mixture of strained yogurt and crème fraîche.

GRILLED NECTARINES WITH RICOTTA AND STAR ANISE

This easy dessert is good at any time of year—use canned peach halves if fresh nectarines are not available.

Preparation time 3 minutes
Cooking time 6–8 minutes

SERVES 4
4 ripe nectarines
½ cup ricotta cheese or fromage frais
1 tablespoon light brown sugar
½ teaspoon ground star anise

1 Cut the nectarines in half and remove the pits.

2 Arrange the nectarines, cut side up, in a wide flameproof dish or on a baking sheet.

COOK'S TIP
Star anise has a warm, rich flavor—if you can't get it, try ground cloves or pumpkin pie spice instead.

3 Put the ricotta or fromage frais in a bowl and stir in the sugar. Using a teaspoon, spoon the mixture into the hollow of each nectarine half. Preheat the broiler.

4 Sprinkle with the star anise. Place under the broiler and broil for 6–8 minutes, or until the nectarines are hot and bubbling. Serve warm.

30-MINUTE RECIPES

If you've cooked your way right through this book, having half an hour at your disposal will seem like unimaginable luxury. The recipes in this section are so deliciously imaginative, however, that you could easily waste ten minutes deciding what to try. Shall it be Turkey Rolls with Gazpacho Sauce, Duck Breasts with Calvados or those scrumptious Sole Goujons with Lime Mayonnaise? Whatever you choose, leave room for a speedy dessert such as Nectarine Puff Pastry Tarts or Amaretto Soufflé.

WATERCRESS AND ORANGE SOUP

This refreshing and healthy soup is great hot or cold.

Preparation time 5 minutes
Cooking time 20 minutes

SERVES 4
1 tablespoon olive oil
1 large onion, chopped
2 bunches of watercress
grated zest and juice of 1 orange
2 ½ cups vegetable stock
⅔ cup light cream
2 teaspoons cornstarch
salt and ground black pepper
a little thick cream, to garnish
4 orange wedges, to serve

1 Heat the oil in a large pan and sauté the onion until softened. Trim any large, thick stalks from the watercress, then add to the pan of onion without chopping. Cover and cook for about 5 minutes.

2 Add the grated orange zest and juice, then pour in the vegetable stock. Bring to a boil, cover, lower the heat and simmer for about 10 minutes. Purée the soup in a blender or food processor. Return it to the pan. Add the cream blended with the cornstarch, and season to taste with salt and pepper.

3 Bring the soup gently back to a boil, stirring until just slightly thickened. Check the seasoning and serve the soup topped with a swirl of cream. Offer a wedge of orange to squeeze in at the last minute.

MUSHROOM AND HERB SOUP

Although you can make mushroom soup with a nice smooth texture, it is more time-consuming and you waste a lot of mushrooms—so enjoy the slightly nutty consistency instead!

Preparation time 5 minutes
Cooking time 20 minutes

SERVES 4

2 ounces sliced bacon
1 white onion, chopped
1 tablespoon sunflower oil
3 cups portobello mushrooms or a mixture of portobello and cremini mushrooms
2½ cups beef stock
2 tablespoons sweet sherry
2 tablespoons chopped, mixed fresh herbs, or 2 teaspoons dried herbs
salt and ground black pepper
4 tablespoons thick plain yogurt or crème fraîche and a few sprigs of marjoram or sage, to garnish

1 | Roughly chop the bacon and place in a large saucepan. Cook gently until all the fat is rendered from the bacon.

2 | Add the onion, with the oil, and cook until softened. Wipe the mushrooms clean, chop them roughly and add to the pan. Cover and cook over low heat until they have softened completely and yielded their liquid.

3 | Add the stock, sherry, herbs and seasoning, cover and simmer for 10–12 minutes. Blend or process the soup until fairly smooth, but with some texture.

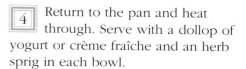

4 | Return to the pan and heat through. Serve with a dollop of yogurt or crème fraîche and an herb sprig in each bowl.

CARROT AND CILANTRO SOUP

Carrot soup is best made with young carrots, when they are at their sweetest and tastiest. With older carrots, you will have to use more to get the full flavor.

Preparation time 5 minutes
Cooking time 20–25 minutes

SERVES 5–6
1 onion, chopped
1 tablespoon sunflower oil
1½ pounds carrots, chopped
3¾ cups chicken stock
few sprigs of cilantro, or
*   1 teaspoon dried coriander*
1 teaspoon lemon zest
2 tablespoons lemon juice
salt and ground black pepper
chopped fresh parsley or cilantro,
*   to garnish*

1 Soften the onion in the oil in a large pan. Add the chopped carrots, stock, cilantro, lemon zest and juice. Season to taste.

2 Bring to a boil, cover and cook for 15–20 minutes. When the carrots are very tender, purée the soup in a blender or food processor, return it to the pan, then check the seasoning.

3 Heat through again and sprinkle with chopped parsley or cilantro before serving.

SHRIMP AND CORN CHOWDER

This quick and easy soup is perfect for informal entertaining.

Preparation time 3 minutes
Cooking time 23 minutes

SERVES 4
1 tablespoon butter
1 onion, chopped
11-ounce can corn
2 tablespoons lemon juice
1¼ cups fish stock
4 ounces cooked, peeled shrimp
1¼ cups milk
1–2 tablespoons light cream
salt and ground black pepper
4 large shrimp in their shells and a
*   few parsley or dill sprigs, to garnish*

1 Heat the butter in a pan and cook the onion until translucent. Add half the corn and all the can liquid, the lemon juice, stock and half the shrimp.

2 Cover and simmer the soup for about 15 minutes, then purée in a food processor or blender.

3 Return the soup to the pan and add the milk. Chop the rest of the shrimp, and add them with the remaining corn and cream. Season to taste with salt and pepper, then cook gently for 5 minutes, or until reduced sufficiently.

4 Ladle the soup into warmed bowls. Serve each portion garnished with a whole shrimp and an herb sprig. Serve with warm ciabatta bread, if you like.

CHINESE GARLIC MUSHROOMS

Tofu is high in protein and very low in cholesterol. It makes a very tasty stuffing for mushrooms.

SERVES 4

Preparation time 5 minutes
Cooking time 15–20 minutes

8 large portobello mushrooms
3 scallions, sliced
1 garlic clove, crushed
2 tablespoons oyster sauce
10½-ounce package marinated tofu,
  cut into small dice
7-ounce can corn, drained
2 teaspoons sesame oil
salt and ground black pepper

1 Preheat the oven to 400°F. Finely chop the mushroom stalks; mix with the scallions, garlic and oyster sauce.

2 Stir in the diced marinated tofu and corn, season well with salt and pepper, then spoon the filling into the mushrooms.

3 Brush the edges of the mushrooms with the sesame oil. Arrange the stuffed mushrooms in a baking dish and bake for 15–20 minutes, until the mushrooms are just tender. Serve at once.

COOK'S TIP
If you prefer, omit the oyster sauce and use light soy sauce instead.

MUSSELS WITH CREAM AND PARSLEY

Preparation time 10–12 minutes
Cooking time 10 minutes

SERVES 2

1½ pounds mussels in the shell
½ fennel bulb, finely chopped
1 shallot, finely chopped
3 tablespoons dry white wine
3 tablespoons light cream
2 tablespoons chopped fresh parsley

1   Scrub the mussels under cold running water. Tear away the beards and discard any that remain open when tapped. Rinse once more.

2   Place the mussels in a large wide pan with a lid. Sprinkle them with the fennel, shallot and wine. Cover and place over medium-high heat, shaking the pan occasionally. Steam for 3–5 minutes, until the mussels open.

3   Lift out the mussels with a slotted spoon and remove the top shells. Discard any that did not open. Arrange the mussels, on their bottom shells, in a shallow serving dish. Cover and keep hot.

4   Place a double layer of dampened cheesecloth or a clean dish towel in a sieve set over a bowl. Strain the mussel cooking liquid through this into a clean saucepan and bring to a boil.

5   Add the cream, stir well and boil for 3 minutes to reduce slightly, then stir in the parsley. Spoon the sauce over the mussels. Sprinkle with pepper, if you like. Serve the mussels immediately.

BEET AND HERRING SALAD

This colorful salad uses fresh beets—too often underrated.

Preparation time 5–6 minutes
Cooking time None

SERVES 4–6
*12 ounces cooked beets, peeled and
  thickly sliced
2 tablespoons vinaigrette dressing
4 rollmop herrings, drained
12 ounces cooked waxy potatoes,
  thickly sliced
½ small red onion, thinly sliced and
  separated into rings
⅔ cup sour cream
2 tablespoons snipped fresh chives
dark rye bread, to serve*

1   Mix the sliced cooked beets with the dressing. Arrange the herrings on individual plates with the beets, potatoes and onion.

2   Add a generous spoonful of the sour cream to each serving and sprinkle with snipped chives. Serve with dark rye bread.

GARLIC SHRIMP IN PHYLLO TARTLETS

Tartlets made with crisp layers of phyllo pastry and filled with garlic shrimp make a tempting appetizer.

Preparation time 8 minutes
Cooking time 10–15 minutes

SERVES 4
*4 tablespoons butter, melted
2–3 large sheets phyllo pastry*
For the filling
*8 tablespoons (1 stick) butter
2–3 garlic cloves, crushed
1 red chile, seeded and chopped
12 ounces cooked, peeled
  large shrimp
2 tablespoons chopped fresh parsley
  or snipped fresh chives
salt and ground black pepper*

1   Preheat the oven to 400°F. Brush four individual 3-inch tart pans with melted butter.

2   Cut the phyllo pastry into twelve 4-inch squares and brush with the melted butter.

3   Place three phyllo pastry squares inside each tart pan, overlapping them at slight angles and carefully frilling the edges and points while forming a good hollow in the center. Bake for 10–15 minutes, until crisp and golden brown.

4   Meanwhile, make the filling. Melt the butter in a large frying pan, and sauté the garlic, chile and shrimp for 1–2 minutes to warm through. Stir in the parsley or chives and season well.

5   Remove the tartlets from the pans and place on individual plates. Spoon in the shrimp filling and serve.

BAKED EGGS WITH CREAMY LEEKS

The French have traditionally enjoyed eggs prepared in many different ways. Vary this simple yet elegant dish by using other vegetables, such as puréed spinach, or ratatouille, as a base.

Preparation time 2 minutes
Cooking time 17–20 minutes

SERVES 4

*1 tablespoon butter, plus extra for
   greasing
8 ounces small leeks, thinly sliced
   (about 2 cups)
5–6 tablespoons whipping cream
freshly grated nutmeg
4 eggs
salt and ground black pepper*

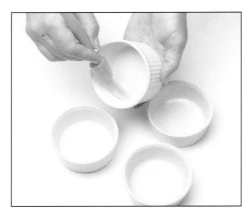

1 Preheat the oven to 375°F. Generously butter the bottom and sides of four ramekins or individual soufflé dishes. Set them aside while you cook the leeks.

2 Melt the butter in a small frying pan and cook the leeks over medium heat, stirring frequently, until softened but not browned.

3 Add 3 tablespoons of the cream and cook gently for 5 minutes, until the leeks are very soft and the cream has thickened a little. Season with salt, pepper and nutmeg.

4 Arrange the ramekins in a small roasting pan and divide the leeks among them. Break an egg into each. Spoon 1–2 teaspoons of the remaining cream over each egg and season lightly.

5 Pour boiling water into the roasting pan to come halfway up the sides of the ramekins. Bake for 10 minutes, until the whites are set and the yolks are still soft, or a little longer if you prefer your eggs a little firmer. Serve at once.

CHEESE-STUFFED PEARS

These pears, with their scrumptious creamy topping, make a sublime dish when served with a simple salad.

Preparation time 5 minutes
Cooking time 23 minutes

SERVES 4

¼ cup ricotta cheese
¼ cup dolcelatte cheese
  (gorgonzola dolce)
1 tablespoon honey
½ celery rib, finely sliced
8 green olives, pitted and chopped
4 dates, pitted and cut into strips
pinch of paprika
4 ripe pears
⅔ cup apple juice
green salad, to serve

1 Preheat the oven to 400ºF. Place the ricotta in a bowl and crumble in the dolcelatte. Add the rest of the ingredients except for the pears and apple juice and mix well.

2 Halve the pears lengthwise and use a melon baller to remove the cores. Place in an ovenproof dish and divide the filling equally between them, piling it up.

3 Pour the apple juice into the dish, taking care not to disturb the filled pears. Cover the dish with foil. Bake for 20 minutes, or until the pears are tender when pierced with a skewer or the point of a sharp knife. Preheat the broiler. Remove the foil from the dish.

4 Place the dish under the hot broiler for about 3 minutes. Serve immediately with green salad.

COOK'S TIP
Choose ripe pears in season such as Bosc, Bartlett or Comice.

TURKEY ROLLS WITH GAZPACHO SAUCE

Cook these wonderful turkey rolls, with their spicy sausage centers, on the grill or under the broiler. The cool, fresh gazpacho sauce is the perfect accompaniment.

Preparation time 8 minutes
Cooking time 10–12 minutes

SERVES 4
4 turkey breast cutlets
1 tablespoon red pesto or tomato paste
4 chorizo sausages
salt and ground black pepper
For the gazpacho sauce
1 green bell pepper, seeded and chopped
1 red bell pepper, seeded and chopped
3-inch piece of cucumber
1 tomato
1 garlic clove, chopped
1 tablespoon red wine vinegar
3 tablespoons olive oil

1. To make the gazpacho sauce, place the peppers, cucumber, tomato, garlic, and vinegar in a food processor. Pour in 2 tablespoons of the oil and process until almost smooth. Season to taste with salt and pepper and set aside.

2. If the turkey breast cutlets are quite thick, place them between two sheets of plastic wrap and beat them with the side of a rolling pin, to flatten them slightly.

3. Spread the pesto or tomato paste over the turkey and then place a chorizo on each piece and roll up firmly. Preheat the broiler or grill.

4. Slice the rolls thickly and thread them onto skewers. Brush with the remaining oil and broil or grill for 10–12 minutes, turning once. Serve with the gazpacho sauce.

CHICKEN IN CREAMY ORANGE SAUCE

This sauce is deceptively creamy—in fact it is made with low-fat fromage frais, which is virtually fat-free. The brandy adds richness.

Preparation time 3–4 minutes
Cooking time 25 minutes

SERVES 4
8 *skinless chicken thighs or drumsticks*
3 *tablespoons brandy*
1¼ *cups orange juice*
3 *scallions, chopped*
2 *teaspoons cornstarch*
6 *tablespoons low-fat fromage frais*
salt and ground black pepper
rice or pasta and green salad, to serve

1 Cook the chicken pieces without fat in a nonstick or heavy pan, turning until they are evenly browned.

2 Stir in the brandy, orange juice and scallions. Bring to a boil, then cover, lower the heat and simmer for 15 minutes, or until the chicken is tender and fully cooked.

3 Blend the cornstarch with a little water, then stir the paste into the fromage frais. Stir this into the sauce and stir over medium heat until the sauce boils and thickens.

4 Adjust the seasoning and serve with boiled rice or pasta and green salad.

COOK'S TIP
Skinless, boneless chicken thighs are perfect for this dish and a host of similar quick lunch or supper dishes. They cook rapidly and have plenty of flavor.

VARIATIONS
To make Turkey in Creamy Orange Sauce, substitute 4 turkey cutlets for the chicken thighs or drumsticks.

TANDOORI CHICKEN KEBABS

This dish comes from the plains of the Punjab at the foot of the Himalayas, where food is traditionally cooked in clay ovens known as tandoors—hence the name.

Preparation time 18 minutes
Cooking time 10–12 minutes

SERVES 4

4 skinless, boneless chicken breasts,
   about 6 ounces each
1 tablespoon lemon juice
3 tablespoons tandoori paste
3 tablespoons plain yogurt
1 garlic clove, crushed
2 tablespoons chopped cilantro
1 small onion, cut into wedges and
   separated into layers
a little oil, for brushing
salt and ground black pepper
cilantro, to garnish
rice pilaf and naan bread, to serve

1. Chop the chicken breasts into 1-inch cubes, place in a bowl and add the lemon juice, tandoori paste, yogurt, garlic, cilantro and seasoning. Mix well. Cover and set aside for 15 minutes.

2. Preheat the broiler. Thread alternate pieces of chicken and onion onto four skewers.

3. Brush the onion with a little oil, lay on a broiler rack and cook under high heat for 10–12 minutes, turning once. Garnish the kebabs with fresh cilantro and serve at once with rice pilaf and naan bread.

COOK'S TIP
You can make your own tandoori paste if you like, but the bought product is a boon to the busy cook.

CHINESE CHICKEN WITH CASHEW NUTS

Preparation time 20 minutes
Cooking time 10 minutes

SERVES 4

4 skinless, boneless chicken breasts,
   sliced into strips
3 garlic cloves, crushed
4 tablespoons soy sauce
2 tablespoons cornstarch
8 ounces dried egg noodles
3 tablespoons sunflower oil
1 tablespoon sesame oil
1 cup roasted cashew nuts
6 scallions, cut into 2-inch pieces and
   halved lengthwise
scallions curls and a little chopped
   red chile, to garnish

1. Place the chicken in a bowl with the garlic, soy sauce and cornstarch. Stir to coat. Cover and chill for 15–18 minutes.

2. Meanwhile, bring a pan of water to a boil and add the egg noodles. Turn off the heat and let stand for 5 minutes. Drain well and reserve.

3. Heat the oils in a large frying pan or wok and add the chilled chicken and marinade juices. Stir-fry over high heat for 3–4 minutes, or until golden brown.

4. Add the cashew nuts and scallions to the pan or wok and stir-fry for 2–3 minutes more.

5. Add the drained noodles and stir-fry for another 2 minutes. Toss the mixture well and serve immediately, garnished with the scallion curls and chopped red chile.

TURKEY STICKS WITH SOUR CREAM DIP

Preparation time 10 minutes
Cooking time 20 minutes

Serves 4
*12 ounces turkey cutlets, or 2 skinless,
  boneless breasts
1 cup fine fresh bread crumbs
¹/₄ teaspoon paprika
1 egg
3 tablespoons sour cream
1 tablespoon tomato sauce
1 tablespoon mayonnaise
salt and ground black pepper
green salad or vegetables, to serve*

1 Preheat the oven to 375°F.
Cut the turkey into strips.
Mix the bread crumbs with paprika.
Season with salt and pepper. Beat
the egg lightly in a shallow bowl.

2 Dip the turkey into the egg,
then into the bread crumbs,
until thoroughly and evenly coated.
Place on a baking sheet.

3 Bake the turkey for 20 minutes,
until crisp and golden. Turn
once during cooking.

4 To make the dip, mix the
sour cream, tomato sauce and
mayonnaise together in a small bowl
and season to taste. Serve the turkey
sticks with baked potatoes
and a green salad or crisp green
vegetables, accompanied by the dip.

CHICKEN, BACON AND CORN KEBABS

*Don't wait for barbecue weather to
serve these colorful kebabs.*

Preparation time 5 minutes
Cooking time 18–20 minutes

Serves 4
*2 ears of corn
8 thick slices lean bacon
8 cremini mushrooms, halved
2 small chicken breast fillets
2 tablespoons sunflower oil
1 tablespoon lemon juice
1 tablespoon maple syrup
salt and ground black pepper
salad, to serve*

1 Cook the corn in boiling water
until tender, then drain and
set aside. Stretch the bacon slices
with the back of a knife; cut each
in half. Wrap a piece around each
half mushroom.

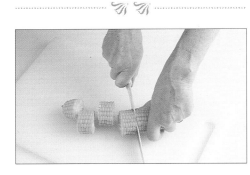

2 Cut both the corn and chicken
into eight equal pieces. Mix the
oil, lemon juice, syrup and seasoning;
brush some over the chicken.

3 Thread the corn, bacon-
wrapped mushrooms and
chicken pieces alternately on skewers
and brush with the lemon dressing.

4 Broil the kebabs for 8–10 minutes, turning once and basting
occasionally with any extra dressing.
Serve hot with either a crisp green or
mixed salad. If serving the kebabs to
children, slide the corn and chicken
off the skewers and serve in pita
breads.

CHICKEN PAELLA

There are many variations of this basic recipe. Any seasonal vegetables can be added, as can mussels or clams. Serve straight from the pan.

Preparation time 3 minutes
Cooking time 25–27 minutes

SERVES 4

4 chicken legs (thighs and
   drumsticks)
¼ cup olive oil
1 large onion, finely chopped
1 garlic clove, crushed
1 teaspoon ground turmeric
4 ounces chorizo sausage or
   smoked ham
generous 1 cup long-grain rice
2½ cups chicken stock
4 tomatoes, peeled, seeded
   and chopped
1 red bell pepper, seeded and sliced
1 cup frozen peas
salt and ground black pepper

COOK'S TIP
Use chicken breasts if you prefer.

1   Preheat the oven to 350ºF. Cut the chicken legs in half. Heat the oil in a 12-inch paella pan or large flameproof casserole and brown the chicken pieces on both sides. Add the onion and garlic and stir in the turmeric. Cook for 2 minutes over medium heat.

2   Slice the sausage or dice the ham and add to the pan, with the rice and stock. Bring to a boil and season to taste, then lower the heat, cover and cook for 10 minutes.

3   Remove from the heat and add the chopped tomatoes, sliced pepper and frozen peas. Return to the heat and cook, stirring frequently, for 10–15 minutes more, or until the chicken is tender and fully cooked and the rice has absorbed the stock.

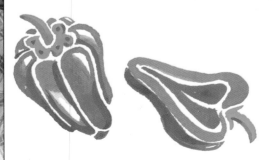

DUCK BREASTS WITH CALVADOS

A plum and Calvados purée is the perfect accompaniment for glazed duck breasts with endive.

Preparation time 5 minutes
Cooking time 25 minutes

SERVES 4
1 tablespoon lemon juice
4 heads of endive
4 duck breasts, about 4 ounces each
1 tablespoon honey
1 teaspoon sunflower oil
salt and ground black pepper

For the purée
1 cooking apple, peeled, cored
    and sliced
6 ounces plums, halved
    and pitted
1 tablespoon light brown sugar
²/₃ cup vegetable stock
3 tablespoons Calvados
2 teaspoons sherry vinegar or red
    wine vinegar

1 Preheat the oven to 425°F. Make the fruit purée. Put the apple, plums, sugar and stock into a saucepan. Bring to a boil, lower the heat and simmer for 10 minutes, until the fruit is very soft. Press the fruit through a strainer into a bowl.

2 Stir the lemon juice into a saucepan of lightly salted water and bring to a boil. Cut the heads of endive lengthwise into quarters and add to the pan. Cook for about 3 minutes, then drain and set aside.

3 Meanwhile, score the duck breasts using a sharp knife, then brush with honey and sprinkle with a little salt. Transfer to a baking sheet and bake for about 6 minutes.

COOK'S TIP
Adding lemon juice to the water used for cooking the endive helps to keep it from discoloring.

4 Brush the endive pieces with oil and place them next to the duck. Bake for 6 minutes more.

5 Stir the Calvados and vinegar into the fruit purée and season to taste with salt and pepper. Arrange the endive pieces on a platter. Slice the duck breasts and fan them out on top of the endive. Spoon the purée over them and serve at once.

PEPPER STEAKS WITH CHIVE BUTTER AND BRANDY

Preparation time 4 minutes
Cooking time 12 minutes

SERVES 4

4 fillet or sirloin beef steaks,
   4–6 ounces each
3 tablespoons olive oil
1 tablespoon black and white
   peppercorns, coarsely crushed
1 garlic clove, halved
4 tablespoons butter
2 tablespoons brandy
1 cup beef stock or consommé
salt and ground black pepper
tied chive bundles, to garnish
boiled new potatoes, to serve

For the chive butter
4 tablespoons butter
3 tablespoons snipped fresh chives

1 Make the chive butter. Beat the butter until soft, add the chives and season with salt and pepper. Beat until well mixed, then shape into a roll, wrap in foil and chill.

2 Brush the steaks with a little olive oil and press crushed peppercorns onto both sides.

3 Rub the cut surface of the garlic over a frying pan. Melt the butter in the remaining oil. When hot, add the steaks and cook quickly, allowing 3½–4 minutes on each side for medium-rare. Lift out with tongs, place on a serving plate and keep hot while you make the sauce.

4 Add the brandy and stock to the pan, boil rapidly until reduced by half, then season with salt and pepper to taste. Slice the chive butter and put a piece on top of each steak. Spoon a little sauce onto each plate. Garnish each steak with a chive bundle and serve with a simple vegetable accompaniment, such as boiled new potatoes.

HAM WITH MADEIRA SAUCE

Preparation time 4 minutes
Cooking time 26 minutes

SERVES 4

2 tablespoons sunflower oil
2 ham steaks, 4–6 ounces each,
   fat snipped to prevent curling
1 onion, sliced
6 ounces (1½ cups) button mushrooms
6 ounces raw beets, peeled and cut
   into thin sticks
salt and ground black pepper
chopped fresh parsley, to garnish

For the sauce
2 tablespoons butter
1 large onion, chopped
1 slice lean bacon, chopped
1 celery rib, diced
2 teaspoons all-purpose flour
2 tomatoes, peeled and diced
1 tablespoon tomato paste
1¼ cups beef stock
1 tablespoon chopped fresh parsley
2 tablespoons Madeira

1 Make the sauce. Heat the butter and sauté the onion, bacon and celery for 5 minutes, until golden. Stir in the flour and cook until browned, then add the tomatoes, tomato paste, stock and parsley. Bring to a boil, then lower the heat and simmer while you cook the ham steaks.

2 Heat the oil in a frying pan and cook the ham steaks with the onion for about 10 minutes, stirring the onion occasionally. Turn the steaks over, add the mushrooms and cook for 10 minutes more, or until the steaks are done.

3 Meanwhile, cook the beet sticks in a pan of lightly salted boiling water for 5 minutes, or until tender. Drain and keep hot.

4 Strain the sauce into a clean pan, stir in the Madeira and season to taste with salt and pepper.

5 Reheat the sauce, pour it over the steaks and serve with the mushrooms, onion and beets. Garnish with the parsley.

COOK'S TIP
Straining the sauce through cheesecloth will give a shiny, glossy finish.

PANFRIED MEDITERRANEAN LAMB

The warm, summery flavors of the Mediterranean are combined for a quick weekday meal.

Preparation time 4 minutes
Cooking time 24 minutes

SERVES 4
8 lean lamb chops
1 medium onion, thinly sliced
2 red bell peppers, seeded and sliced
14-ounce can whole peeled plum tomatoes
1 garlic clove, crushed
3 tablespoons chopped fresh basil leaves
2 tablespoons chopped black olives

1 Trim any excess fat from the lamb, then cook without fat in a nonstick pan until golden brown.

2 Add the onion and peppers to the pan. Cook, stirring, for a few minutes to soften, then add the plum tomatoes, garlic and basil.

3 Simmer for 20 minutes, or until the lamb is tender. Stir in the olives, season, and serve.

VARIATIONS
This recipe would be equally good with skinless chicken breast fillets instead of the lamb chops. Or use cod steaks, which are very good with a robust tomato sauce.

BACON KOFTAS

These easy koftas are good for outdoor summer barbecues, served with lots of salad.

Preparation time 15 minutes
Cooking time 8–10 minutes

SERVES 4
8 ounces lean bacon, coarsely chopped
1 cup fresh whole-wheat bread crumbs
2 scallions, chopped
1 tablespoon chopped fresh parsley
finely grated zest of 1 lemon
1 egg white
ground mixed peppercorns
paprika
lemon zest and fresh parsley leaves, to garnish
lemon rice and salad, to serve

1 Place the bacon in a food processor together with the bread crumbs, scallions, parsley, lemon zest, egg white and peppercorns. Process the mixture until it is finely chopped and begins to bind together, but do not let it form a paste.

2 Divide the bacon mixture into eight even-size pieces and shape into long ovals around eight wooden or bamboo skewers. The easiest way to do this is to use your hands. Preheat the broiler or grill.

3 Sprinkle the koftas with paprika and cook under the hot broiler or on the grill for 8–10 minutes, turning occasionally, until browned and cooked through. Garnish with lemon zest and parsley leaves, then serve hot with lemon rice and salad.

COOK'S TIPS
Don't overprocess the kofta mixture; it should be only just mixed. If you don't have a food processor, either grind the bacon, or chop it very finely by hand, then mix it with the rest of the ingredients.

SKEWERED LAMB WITH CUCUMBER RAITA

Lamb is the most commonly used meat for Turkish kebabs, but lean beef or pork work equally well. For color you can alternate pieces of pepper, lemon or onions, although this is not traditional.

Preparation time 15 minutes
Cooking time 10 minutes

SERVES 4
2 pounds lean boneless lamb
1 large onion, grated
3 bay leaves
5 thyme or rosemary sprigs
grated zest and juice of 1 lemon
$\frac{1}{2}$ teaspoon sugar
$\frac{1}{3}$ cup olive oil
salt and ground black pepper
sprigs of rosemary, to garnish
broiled lemon wedges, to serve

For the cucumber raita
$\frac{1}{2}$ cucumber
1 green chile, seeded and chopped
$1\frac{1}{4}$ cups strained plain yogurt
$\frac{1}{4}$ teaspoon salt
$\frac{1}{4}$ teaspoon ground cumin

1 │ To make the kebabs, cut the lamb into small chunks and place in a bowl. Mix together the grated onion, herbs, lemon zest and juice, sugar and oil, then add salt and pepper and pour over the lamb.

2 │ Mix the ingredients together and let marinate in the refrigerator while you make the raita.

COOK'S TIP
Cover the tips of wooden skewers with foil so they don't char.

3 │ Dice the cucumber finely and place in a bowl. Stir in the chopped chile.

4 │ Add the yogurt, salt and ground cumin. Preheat the broiler.

5 │ Drain the meat and thread it onto skewers. Broil for 10 minutes, until browned, turning twice. Garnish with the rosemary and broiled lemon wedges and serve with the raita.

PORK AND PINEAPPLE SATAY

This variation on the classic satay has added pineapple, but keeps the traditional coconut and peanut sauce. It is very easy to make and tastes delicious.

Preparation time 5–8 minutes
Cooking time 15 minutes

SERVES 4

1¼ pounds pork tenderloin
1 small onion, chopped
1 garlic clove, chopped
¼ cup soy sauce
finely grated zest of ½ lemon
1 teaspoon ground cumin
1 teaspoon ground coriander
1 teaspoon ground turmeric
1 teaspoon dark brown sugar
8-ounce can pineapple chunks, or
   1 small fresh pineapple, peeled
   and diced
parsley, to garnish

For the satay sauce
¾ cup coconut milk
⅓ cup crunchy peanut butter
1 garlic clove, crushed
2 teaspoons soy sauce
1 teaspoon dark brown sugar

1 Trim any fat from the pork and cut it into 1-inch cubes. Place the meat in a large bowl.

2 Place the onion, garlic, soy sauce, lemon zest, spices and sugar in a blender or food processor. Add two pieces of pineapple and process until the mixture is well combined and almost smooth.

3 Mix the paste and the pork, tossing well to coat evenly. Thread the pieces of pork onto bamboo skewers with the remaining pineapple chunks. Preheat the broiler or light the grill.

4 To make the sauce, pour the coconut milk into a small pan and stir in the peanut butter. Stir in all the remaining sauce ingredients and heat gently on the stove or over the grill, stirring until smooth and hot. Cover and keep warm.

5 Cook the pork and pineapple skewers under the broiler or on a medium-hot grill for 10–12 minutes, turning occasionally, until golden brown and thoroughly cooked. Garnish with parsley and serve with the satay sauce.

FRIED RICE WITH PORK

If you like, garnish the fried rice with strips of omelet.

Preparation time 16 minutes
Cooking time 10 minutes

SERVES 4–6
1 cup long-grain rice
3 tablespoons vegetable oil
1 onion, chopped
1 tablespoon chopped garlic
4 ounces pork, cut into small cubes
2 eggs, beaten
2 tablespoons fish sauce
1 tablespoon dark soy sauce
$1/2$ teaspoon sugar
For the garnish
4 scallions, finely sliced
2 red chiles, sliced
1 lime, cut into wedges

1 Cook the rice in boiling salted water for 11 minutes. Heat the oil in a wok or frying pan. Add the onion and garlic.

2 Cook the onion and garlic for 2 minutes, then add the pork and stir-fry until it is cooked.

3 Add the eggs and cook until scrambled into small lumps.

4 Add the rice and continue to stir and toss, to coat it with the oil and prevent it from sticking.

5 Stir in the fish sauce, soy sauce and sugar and mix well. Continue to fry until the rice is thoroughly heated. Place in a bowl and garnish with sliced scallion, red chiles and lime wedges. Top with a few strips of omelet, if you like.

BEEF AND MUSHROOM BURGERS

It's worth making your own burgers to cut down on fat—in these the meat is extended with mushrooms for extra fiber.

Preparation time 7 minutes
Cooking time 12–15 minutes

SERVES 4

5 ounces (1¼ cups) small mushrooms
1 small onion, chopped
1 pound lean ground beef
1 cup fresh whole-wheat
  bread crumbs
1 teaspoon dried mixed herbs
1 tablespoon tomato paste
all-purpose flour, for shaping
salt and ground black pepper

1 Place the mushrooms and onion in a food processor and process until finely chopped. Add the beef, bread crumbs, herbs and tomato paste. Season. Process until the mixture binds together but still has some texture.

2 Divide the mixture into 8–10 pieces, then press into patties using lightly floured hands.

3 Cook the burgers in a nonstick frying pan or under a hot broiler for 12–15 minutes, turning once, until evenly cooked. Serve with relish and lettuce, in hamburger buns or pita bread.

COOK'S TIP
The mixture is soft, so handle carefully and use a spatula for turning to keep the burgers from breaking during cooking.

PROSCIUTTO, MUSHROOM AND ARTICHOKE PIZZA

Here is a pizza full of rich and varied flavors. For a delicious variation, use mixed cultivated and wild mushrooms.

Preparation time 3 minutes
Cooking time 20–25 minutes

SERVES 2–3
1 bunch scallions
4 tablespoons olive oil
8 ounces (2 cups) mushrooms, sliced
2 garlic cloves, chopped
1 pizza crust, about 10–12-inches in
    diameter
8 slices prosciutto
4 artichoke hearts in oil,
    drained and sliced
¼ cup freshly grated Parmesan
salt and ground black pepper
thyme sprigs, to garnish

1 Preheat the oven to 425°F. Trim the scallions, then chop all the white and some of the green stems.

2 Heat 2 tablespoons of the oil in a frying pan. Add the scallions, mushrooms and garlic and sauté over medium heat until all the juices have evaporated. Season and let cool.

3 Brush the pizza crust with half the remaining oil. Arrange the prosciutto, mushroom mixture and artichoke hearts on top.

4 Sprinkle the Parmesan over the pizza, then drizzle with the remaining oil. Bake for 15–20 minutes. Garnish with thyme and serve.

MIXED SEAFOOD PIZZA

Here is a pizza that gives you the full flavor of the Mediterranean, ideal for a summer evening supper!

Preparation time 5 minutes
Cooking time 15–20 minutes

SERVES 3–4

1 pizza crust, 10–12-inches in
    diameter
2 tablespoons olive oil
1 cup good-quality pasta sauce
14 ounces mixed cooked seafood, such
    as shrimps, squid, and mussels
3 garlic cloves
2 tablespoons chopped fresh parsley
2 tablespoons freshly grated
    Parmesan cheese, to serve

VARIATION

If you prefer, this pizza can be made with either mussels or shrimp on their own, or any combination of your favorite seafood.

1   Preheat the oven to 425°F. Lightly brush the top of the pizza crust with about 1 tablespoon of the olive oil.

2   Spread the pasta sauce over it. Bake for 10 minutes.

3   Pat the seafood dry using paper towels, then arrange on top of the pizza.

4   Finely chop the garlic and sprinkle it evenly over the surface, then sprinkle on the chopped fresh parsley.

5   Drizzle the remaining oil over the top and return the pizza to the oven. Bake for 5–10 minutes, until the seafood is warmed through and the crust is crisp and golden. Sprinkle generously with freshly grated Parmesan cheese and serve immediately.

PINEAPPLE CURRY WITH SHRIMP AND MUSSELS

The delicate sweet and sour flavor of this curry comes from the pineapple, and although it seems an odd combination, it is delicious. Use the freshest shellfish you can find.

Preparation time 15 minutes
Cooking time 10 minutes

SERVES 4–6
2¹/₂ cups coconut milk
2 tablespoons red curry paste
2 tablespoons fish sauce
1 tablespoon sugar
8 ounces raw large shrimp, shelled and deveined
1 pound live mussels, cleaned and beards removed
6 ounces fresh pineapple, finely crushed or chopped
5 kaffir lime leaves
2 red chiles, chopped, and cilantro leaves, to garnish

1 In a large saucepan, bring half the coconut milk to a boil. Heat, stirring, until it separates.

2 Add the red curry paste and cook until fragrant. Add the fish sauce and sugar and continue to cook for about 1 minute.

3 Stir in the rest of the coconut milk and bring back to a boil. Add the shrimp, mussels and pineapple. Tear the kaffir lime leaves into pieces and stir them into the mixture.

4 Reheat until boiling, then lower the heat and simmer for 3–5 minutes, until the shrimp are cooked and the mussels have opened. Remove any mussels that have not opened and discard. Spoon into a serving dish, garnish with chopped red chiles and cilantro leaves and serve.

COOK'S TIP
To save time, use drained canned crushed pineapple instead of fresh.

CURRIED SHRIMP IN COCONUT MILK

Preparation time 4 minutes
Cooking time 22 minutes

SERVES 4–6
2¹/₂ cups coconut milk
2 tablespoons yellow curry paste (see Cook's Tip)
1 tablespoon fish sauce
¹/₂ teaspoon salt
1 teaspoon sugar
1 pound raw large shrimp, shelled, tails left intact, and deveined
8 ounces cherry tomatoes
juice of ¹/₂ lime, to serve
For the garnish
2 red chiles, cut into strips
cilantro leaves

1 Put half the coconut milk in a pan or wok and bring to a boil over medium heat.

2 Add the yellow curry paste to the warmed coconut milk, stir until it dissolves, then simmer for about 10 minutes. Add the fish sauce, salt, sugar and remaining coconut milk. Simmer for 5 minutes more, or until the sauce thickens.

3 Add the shrimp and cherry tomatoes. Simmer very gently for about 5 minutes, until the shrimp are pink and tender.

4 Serve sprinkled with lime juice and garnished with chiles and cilantro leaves.

COOK'S TIP
To make yellow curry paste, process together 6–8 yellow chiles, 1 chopped lemongrass stalk, 4 peeled shallots, 4 garlic cloves, 1 tablespoon peeled chopped fresh ginger root, 1 teaspoon coriander seeds, 1 teaspoon mustard powder, 1 teaspoon salt, ¹/₂ teaspoon ground cinnamon, 1 tablespoon light brown sugar and 2 tablespoons oil in a blender or food processor. When a paste has formed, transfer to a glass jar and keep in the refrigerator.

PANFRIED TROUT WITH HAZELNUTS

Hazelnuts make an interesting topping for trout.

Preparation and cooking time 30 minutes

SERVES 4

½ cup shelled hazelnuts, chopped
6 tablespoons butter
4 trout, about 10 ounces each
2 tablespoons lemon juice
salt and ground black pepper
lemon slices and flat-leaf parsley
   sprigs, to garnish

1 Preheat the broiler. Toast the hazelnuts in a single layer, stirring frequently, until the skins split. Then put them on a clean dish towel and rub to remove the skins. Let the hazelnuts cool, then chop them coarsely.

2 Heat 4 tablespoons of the butter in a large frying pan. Season the trout inside and out, then fry two at a time for 12 minutes, turning once, until the trout are brown and the flesh flakes easily when tested with the tip of a sharp knife.

COOK'S TIP

You can use a microwave to prepare the nuts. Spread them in a shallow dish and cook on full power until the skins split. Watch them closely, as they scorch readily.

3 Drain the cooked trout on paper towels, then transfer to a warm serving plate and keep hot while frying the remaining trout in the same way. (If your frying pan is large enough, you could, of course, cook the trout in one batch.) When batch frying, it may be necessary to add a little more butter to the frying pan.

4 Add the remaining butter to the frying pan, then add the hazelnuts and fry them until evenly browned. Stir the lemon juice into the pan and mix well, then quickly pour the buttery sauce over the trout and serve at once, garnished with slices of lemon and flat-leaf parsley sprigs.

PASTA WITH SCALLOPS IN TOMATO SAUCE

Preparation time 6 minutes
Cooking time 17 minutes

Serves 4
1 pound pasta, such as fettuccine
  or linguine
2 tablespoons olive oil
2 garlic cloves, finely chopped
1 pound scallops, sliced in half
  horizontally
2 tablespoons chopped fresh basil
salt and ground black pepper
fresh basil sprigs, to garnish
For the sauce
2 tablespoons olive oil
1/2 onion, finely chopped
1 garlic clove, finely chopped
salt, to taste
2 x 14-ounce cans peeled tomatoes

VARIATION
Substitute 10 peeled fresh plum tomatoes
for the canned tomatoes, if you like.

1 To make the sauce, heat the oil in a nonstick frying pan. Add the onion, garlic and a little salt, and cook over medium heat for about 3 minutes, stirring occasionally.

2 Add the tomatoes, with their juice, and crush with a fork. Bring to a boil, then reduce the heat and simmer while you cook the pasta.

3 Bring a large pan of salted water to a boil. Add the pasta and cook for about 10 minutes, until just tender.

4 Meanwhile, combine the oil and garlic in another nonstick frying pan and cook for about 30 seconds, until just sizzling. Add the scallops and 1/2 teaspoon salt and toss over high heat for about 3 minutes, until they are cooked.

5 Reheat the tomato sauce, add the scallops and season to taste. Keep warm over very low heat.

6 Drain the pasta, place in a bowl and toss with the scallop sauce and the basil. Garnish with basil sprigs and serve.

SOLE GOUJONS WITH LIME MAYONNAISE

This simple dish can be rustled up very quickly. It makes an excellent light lunch or supper.

Preparation time 5–7 minutes
Cooking time 10 minutes

SERVES 4
1 cup mayonnaise
1 small garlic clove, crushed
2 teaspoons capers, rinsed
* and chopped*
2 teaspoons chopped gherkins
finely grated zest of ¹/₂ lime
2 teaspoons lime juice
1 tablespoon chopped cilantro
1¹/₂ pounds sole fillets, skinned
2 eggs, beaten
2 cups fresh white bread crumbs
oil, for deep-frying
salt and ground black pepper
lime wedges, to serve

1 To make the lime mayonnaise, mix together the mayonnaise, garlic, capers, gherkins, lime zest and juice and chopped cilantro. Season with salt and pepper. Transfer to a serving bowl.

2 Cut the sole fillets into finger-length strips. Dip into the beaten egg, then into the fresh white bread crumbs.

3 Heat the oil in a deep-fat fryer to 350°F. Add the fish in batches and fry until golden brown and crisp. Drain on paper towels.

4 Pile the goujons onto warmed serving plates and serve with the lime wedges for squeezing over them. Pass the lime mayonnaise around separately.

SPICY FISH RÖSTI

Serve these fish cakes crisp and hot for lunch with a green salad.

Preparation time 4 minutes
Cooking time 20 minutes

SERVES 4
12 ounces large, firm
* waxy potatoes*
12 ounces salmon or cod fillet,
* skinned, stray bones removed*
3–4 scallions, finely chopped
1 teaspoon grated fresh ginger root
2 tablespoons chopped cilantro
2 teaspoon lemon juice
3 tablespoons sunflower oil
salt and cayenne pepper
lemon wedges, to serve

1 Cook the potatoes with their skins on in a pan of boiling salted water for 10 minutes. Drain and let cool for a few minutes.

2 Meanwhile, finely chop the salmon or cod fillet and place in a bowl. Stir in the scallions, ginger, cilantro and lemon juice. Season with salt and cayenne.

3 When the potatoes are cool enough to handle, peel off the skins and grate the potatoes coarsely. Gently stir the grated potato into the fish mixture.

4 Form the fish and potato mixture into 12 cakes.

5 Heat the oil in a large frying pan, and, when hot, sauté the fish cakes a few at a time for 3 minutes on each side, until golden brown and crisp. Drain on paper towels. Serve hot with lemon wedges for squeezing over. Garnish with sprigs of cilantro, if you like.

TUNA STEAKS WITH PANFRIED PLUM TOMATOES

Preparation time 15–20 minutes
Cooking time 8–10 minutes

SERVES 2

2 tuna steaks, about 6 ounces each
6 tablespoons olive oil
2 tablespoons lemon juice
2 garlic cloves, chopped
1 teaspoon chopped fresh thyme
4 drained canned anchovy fillets,
 finely chopped
8 ounces plum tomatoes, halved
2 tablespoons chopped fresh parsley
4–6 black olives, pitted and chopped
ground black pepper
crusty bread, to serve

COOK'S TIP
If you are unable to find fresh tuna steaks, you could replace them with salmon fillets, if you like—just cook them for one or two minutes more on each side.

1. Place the tuna steaks in a shallow nonreactive dish. Mix 4 tablespoons of the oil with the lemon juice, garlic, thyme, anchovies and pepper. Pour this mixture over the tuna and let marinate for at least 15 minutes, longer if possible.

2. Lift the tuna from the marinade and place on a broiler rack. Broil, basting with the marinade, for 4 minutes on each side, or until the tuna feels firm to the touch.

3. Meanwhile, heat the remaining oil in a frying pan. Sauté the tomatoes briefly on each side.

4. Divide the tomatoes equally between two serving plates and sprinkle the chopped parsley and olives over them. Top each with a tuna steak.

5. Add the remaining marinade to the pan juices and warm through. Pour over the tomatoes and tuna steaks and serve at once with crusty bread for mopping up the delectable juices.

BROILED SEA BASS WITH FENNEL

Fish and fennel are a famous—and delicious—combination.

Preparation time 2 minutes
Cooking time 28 minutes

SERVES 6–8
1 sea bass, weighing 4–4¹/₂ pounds, cleaned
4–6 tablespoons olive oil
2–3 teaspoons fennel seeds
2 large fennel bulbs
¹/₄ cup Pernod
salt and ground black pepper

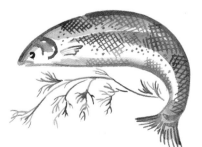

1 With a sharp knife, make three or four deep cuts in both sides of the fish. Brush the fish with olive oil and season with salt and pepper. Sprinkle the fennel seeds in the stomach cavity and cuts. Set aside.

2 Trim the fennel bulbs, saving any fronds. Quarter the bulbs, remove the cores and slice thinly.

3 Preheat the broiler. Put the slices of fennel in a flameproof dish or on the broiler rack and brush with oil. Broil for 4 minutes on each side, until tender. Transfer to a large platter and keep hot.

4 Place the fish on the oiled broiler rack and position 4–5 inches away from the heat. Broil for 10 minutes on each side, brushing with oil occasionally.

5 Transfer the fish to the platter on top of the fennel. Garnish with fennel fronds. Heat the Pernod in a small pan, light it and pour it, flaming, over the fish. Serve at once.

Kashmiri Coconut Fish Curry

Preparation time 6 minutes
Cooking time 20–24 minutes

Serves 4
2 tablespoons vegetable oil
2 onions, sliced
1 green bell pepper, seeded and sliced
1 garlic clove, crushed
1 dried chile, seeded and chopped
1 teaspoon ground coriander
1 teaspoon ground cumin
½ teaspoon ground turmeric
½ teaspoon hot chili powder
½ teaspoon garam masala
1 tablespoon all-purpose flour
¼ cup coconut cream
2½ cups boiling water
1½ pounds haddock fillet
4 tomatoes, peeled, seeded
   and chopped
1 tablespoon lemon juice
2 tablespoons ground almonds
2 tablespoons heavy cream
cilantro sprigs, to garnish
naan bread and boiled rice, to serve

1 Heat the oil in a large saucepan and add the onions, pepper and garlic. Cook for 6–7 minutes, until the onions and pepper have softened. Stir in the chopped dried chile, all the ground spices and the flour. Cook for 1 minute.

2 Pour the coconut in the boiling water and stir into the spicy vegetable mixture. Bring to a boil, cover, lower the heat and simmer gently for 6 minutes.

3 Skin the fish and chop the flesh roughly. Add the fish and tomatoes to the pan and cook for 5–6 minutes, or until the fish has turned opaque. Uncover and gently stir in the lemon juice, ground almonds and cream. Season well, garnish with cilantro and serve with naan bread and rice.

Variations
Replace the haddock with any firm-fleshed white fish such as cod or whiting. Stir in a few cooked, peeled shrimp, if you like.

Mussels with Wine and Garlic

This famous French dish is better known as moules marinière.

Preparation time 10 minutes
Cooking time 12 minutes

Serves 4
4–4½ pounds live mussels
1 tablespoon oil
2 tablespoons butter
1 small onion or 2 shallots, finely
   chopped
2 garlic cloves, finely chopped
⅔ cup dry white wine or cider
fresh parsley sprigs
ground black pepper
2 tablespoons chopped fresh parsley,
   to garnish
French bread, to serve

1 Check that the mussels are closed. (Throw away any that are cracked or won't close when tapped.) Scrape the shells under cold running water and pull off the hairy beard attached to the hinge of the shell. Rinse well several times.

2 Heat the oil and butter in a large pan, add the onions or shallots and garlic and sauté for 3–4 minutes, until softened.

3 Add the wine or cider and the parsley sprigs. Stir well, bring to a boil, then add the mussels. Cover and cook for 5–7 minutes, shaking the pan once or twice, until the shells open (throw away any that stay shut).

4 Place the mussels and their juices in a bowl and top with chopped parsley and black pepper. Serve with hot French bread.

SEAFOOD SALAD PROVENÇALE

You can't beat this salad for an almost instant appetizer or main course, and it is the perfect choice for a buffet table because it keeps so well.

Preparation time 25 minutes
Cooking time None

SERVES 4

12 ounces mixed cooked seafood, such as peeled shrimp, mussels and crabsticks
2 tablespoons tomato sauce
1 garlic clove, crushed
¼ cup pimiento antipasto
¼ cup artichoke antipasto
½ yellow bell pepper, seeded and sliced
lemon juice, to taste
2 tablespoons white wine (optional)
salt and ground black pepper
2 tablespoons chopped fresh parsley and whole shrimp, to garnish

1 Toss the seafood in the tomato sauce, add the garlic and let stand for 5–10 minutes.

2 Mix the pimiento antipasto with the artichoke antipasto, pepper, lemon juice and wine, if using.

3 Stir in the seafood mixture, season to taste, and chill for 15 minutes or longer. Sprinkle with parsley and garnish with shrimp before serving.

MONKFISH AND POTATO KEBABS

Monkfish is a good, firm fish. It works well for kebabs and can be cooked over a fierce heat.

Preparation time 20–25 minutes
Cooking time 4–5 minutes

SERVES 4

12–16 small new potatoes
12–16 seedless grapes
4-inch piece cucumber, cubed
10–12 ounces monkfish tail, boned and cubed
6 tablespoons butter
grated zest and juice of 1 lime
1 teaspoon grated fresh ginger root
1 tablespoon chopped fresh parsley
3–4 tablespoons white wine
salt and ground black pepper
salad, to serve

 1 Boil the potatoes, then arrange on skewers with the grapes, cucumber and monkfish cubes.

2 Melt 4 tablespoons of the butter and stir in the lime zest and juice, ginger, seasoning and half the parsley. Brush some over the kebabs.

3 Preheat the broiler and cook the kebabs, in a dish or on a sheet of foil to catch all the juices, for 2 minutes on each side.

4 When cooked, transfer the kebabs to hot plates while heating the juices with the wine and the remaining butter. Check the seasoning, sprinkle the kebabs with parsley and serve with a salad and the tangy lime sauce.

LEMONGRASS SHRIMP ON CRISP NOODLE CAKE

Preparation time 10 minutes
Cooking time 15 minutes

SERVES 4

11 ounces thin egg noodles
1/4 cup vegetable oil
1 1/4 pounds raw large shrimp, peeled
   and deveined
1/2 teaspoon ground coriander
1 tablespoon ground turmeric
2 garlic cloves, finely chopped
2 slices fresh ginger root,
   finely chopped
2 lemongrass stalks, finely chopped
2 shallots, finely chopped
1 tablespoon tomato paste
1 cup coconut cream
1–2 tablespoons fresh lime juice
1–2 tablespoons fish sauce
4–6 kaffir lime leaves (optional)
1 cucumber, peeled, seeded and cut
   into 2-inch sticks
1 tomato, seeded and cut into strips
2 red chiles, seeded and finely sliced
salt and ground black pepper
finely sliced scallions, and a few
   cilantro sprigs, to garnish

1   Cook the egg noodles in a saucepan of boiling water until just tender. Drain, rinse under cold running water and drain well.

2   Heat 1 tablespoon of the oil in a large frying pan. Add the noodles, distributing them evenly, and fry for 4–5 minutes, until crisp and golden. Turn the noodle cake over and fry the other side. Alternatively, make four individual cakes. Keep hot.

3   Toss the shrimp with the ground spices, garlic, ginger and lemongrass. Season.

4   Heat the remaining oil in a large frying pan. Fry the shallots for 1 minute, then add the shrimp and fry for 2 minutes more. Lift out the shrimp.

5   Stir the tomato paste and coconut cream into the mixture remaining in the pan. Stir in lime juice to taste and season with the fish sauce. Bring the sauce to a simmer, return the shrimp to the sauce, then add the kaffir lime leaves, if using, and the cucumber. Simmer gently until the shrimp are cooked and the sauce is a nice coating consistency.

6   Add the tomato, stir until just warmed through, then add the chiles. Serve on top of the crisp noodle cake(s), garnished with sliced scallions and cilantro sprigs.

SMOKED TROUT PILAF

Preparation time 5 minutes
Cooking time 25 minutes

SERVES 4

1¼ cups white basmati or long-grain
   rice
3 tablespoons butter
2 onions, sliced into rings
1 garlic clove, crushed
2 bay leaves
2 whole cloves
2 green cardamom pods
2 cinnamon sticks
1 teaspoon cumin seeds
2½ cups boiling water
4 smoked trout fillets, skinned
½ cup slivered almonds, toasted
⅓ cup raisins
2 tablespoons chopped fresh
   parsley
mango chutney and pappadams,
   to serve

 1 Wash the rice thoroughly in several changes of water and drain well. Melt the butter in a large frying pan and sauté the onions until well browned, stirring often.

2 Add the garlic, bay leaves and spices. Stir-fry for 1 minute.

3 Stir in the rice, then the boiling water. Bring to a boil. Cover the pan, reduce the heat and cook very gently for 20 minutes, until the water has been absorbed and the rice is tender.

4 Flake the smoked trout and add to the pan with the almonds and raisins. Mix thoroughly. Replace the lid and allow the smoked trout to warm for a few minutes. Sprinkle with the parsley and serve with mango chutney and pappadams.

CRUNCHY-TOPPED COD

Preparation time 4 minutes
Cooking time 15–20 minutes

SERVES 4
4 pieces cod fillet, about 4 ounces
    each, skinned
2 medium tomatoes, sliced
1 cup fresh whole-wheat bread
    crumbs
2 tablespoons chopped fresh parsley
1 teaspoon sunflower oil
finely grated zest and juice of
    ½ lemon
salt and ground black pepper

1 Preheat the oven to 400°F.
    Arrange the cod fillets in a
wide ovenproof dish.

2 Arrange the tomato slices on
    top. Mix the bread crumbs,
fresh parsley, oil, lemon zest and
juice. Season to taste.

3 Spoon the crumb mixture
    evenly over the fish, then bake
for 15–20 minutes. Serve hot.

COOK'S TIP
Choose firm, ripe tomatoes with plenty
of flavor. In the summer you may be
fortunate enough to find fresh plum
tomatoes, which are perfect for this
tasty dish.

CRUMBLY FISH AND SHRIMP PIE

*This fish pie is very easy to make.
For a more economical version, omit
the shrimp and replace with more
fish fillets.*

Preparation time 5 minutes
Cooking time 25 minutes

SERVES 4
12 ounces haddock fillet, skinned
2 tablespoons cornstarch
4 ounces cooked, peeled shrimp
7-ounce can corn, drained
¾ cup frozen peas
⅔ cup milk
⅔ cup fromage frais
1 cup fresh whole-wheat bread
    crumbs
½ cup grated Cheddar cheese
salt and ground black pepper
fresh vegetables, to serve

1 Preheat the oven to 375°F.
    Cut the fish fillets into
bite-size pieces and toss with
the cornstarch.

2 Mix together the fish, shrimp,
    corn and peas in a baking dish.
Combine the milk and fromage frais,
season and pour into the dish.

3 Mix together the bread crumbs
    and grated cheese, then spoon
evenly over the top. Bake for about
25 minutes, or until golden brown.
Serve hot, with fresh vegetables.

COOK'S TIP
This quick recipe can be prepared well
ahead and chilled—keep the bread
crumb topping separately, sprinkling
it over the fish and shrimp mixture just
before baking.

Salmon, Zucchini and Corn Frittata

*A delicious and exciting change
from an omelet, but almost as fast.
Serve this filling frittata with a
mixed tomato and pepper salad and
warm whole-wheat rolls.*

Preparation time 10 minutes
Cooking time 16 minutes

Serves 4–6
2 teaspoons olive oil
1 onion, chopped
6 ounces zucchini, thinly sliced
8 ounces boiled potatoes in their
    skins, cut into chunks
3 eggs, plus 2 egg whites
2 tablespoons milk
7-ounce can pink salmon in brine,
    drained and flaked
7-ounce can corn, drained
2 teaspoons dried mixed herbs
½ cup finely grated aged Cheddar
    cheese
salt and ground black pepper
chopped fresh mixed herbs and basil
    leaves, to garnish
thinly sliced tomatoes and strips of
    red, yellow and green bell pepper,
    to serve

1 Heat the oil in a large nonstick
   frying pan. Add the onion and
sauté for 2 minutes over medium
heat, then stir in the thinly sliced
zucchini and cook for 3 minutes,
stirring the mixture occasionally.

2 Add the potatoes and cook for
   5 minutes, stirring occasionally.

3 Beat the eggs, egg whites and
   milk together, add the salmon,
corn, herbs and seasoning and pour
the mixture evenly over the
vegetables.

4 Cook over medium heat until
   the eggs are beginning to set
and are golden brown underneath.

5 Preheat the broiler. Sprinkle the
   cheese over the frittata and
place it under medium heat until the
cheese has melted and the top is
golden brown.

6 Sprinkle with chopped fresh
   herbs, cut into wedges and
serve immediately, garnished with
basil leaves and accompanied by
sliced tomatoes and mixed peppers.

Cook's Tip
For a reduced-fat version of the frittata,
use low-fat milk and Edam or reduced-
fat Cheddar cheese.

MIXED VEGETABLES WITH AROMATIC SPICES

Transform a selection of everyday vegetables by tossing them with a mixture of fried ginger and aromatic spices.

Preparation time 6 minutes
Cooking time 24 minutes

SERVES 4–6
1½ pounds small new potatoes
1 small cauliflower
6 ounces green beans
1 cup frozen peas
small piece of fresh ginger root
2 tablespoons sunflower oil
2 teaspoons cumin seeds
2 teaspoons black mustard seeds
2 tablespoons sesame seeds
juice of 1 lemon
ground black pepper
cilantro, to garnish (optional)

1 Scrub the potatoes, cut the cauliflower into small florets, and trim and halve the beans. Cook the vegetables in separate pans of lightly salted boiling water until tender, allowing 15–20 minutes for the potatoes, 8 minutes for the cauliflower and 4 minutes for the beans and peas. Drain thoroughly.

2 Using a small, sharp knife, peel and finely chop the fresh ginger. Heat the oil. Add the ginger and seeds. Cook until they start to pop.

3 Add the vegetables and stir-fry for 2–3 minutes. Sprinkle the lemon juice over them and season with pepper. Garnish with cilantro, if using.

COOK'S TIP
Other vegetables could be used, such as zucchini, leeks or broccoli. Buy whatever looks freshest and do not store vegetables for long periods, as their vitamin content will deteriorate.

EGGS WITH SPINACH AND CHEESE SAUCE

To save time, use 1 pound of thawed frozen spinach. There's no need to precook it; just squeeze out the surplus liquid and add it in step 4.

Preparation time 16 minutes
Cooking time 10–12 minutes

SERVES 4

*2 ¼ pounds fresh spinach, stalks
  removed*
3 tablespoons butter
3 tablespoons all-purpose flour
1 ¼ cups milk
¾ cup grated aged Cheddar cheese
pinch of mustard powder
large pinch of freshly grated nutmeg
*4 hard-boiled eggs, peeled and
  halved lengthwise*
salt and ground black pepper

1. Wash but do not dry the spinach, then place in a large saucepan with just the water clinging to the leaves. Cover and cook for 1–2 minutes, until the spinach is just wilted and no liquid is visible. Pour the spinach into a sieve and squeeze out as much liquid as possible, then chop it.

2. Melt 2 tablespoons of the butter in a saucepan, stir in the flour and cook for 1 minute. Gradually add the milk, stirring until the sauce boils and thickens. Lower the heat and simmer for 4 minutes.

3. Remove the pan from the heat and stir in ½ cup of the cheese, the mustard powder and seasoning. Preheat the broiler.

4. Melt the remaining butter in a small saucepan, then stir in the spinach, nutmeg and seasoning and warm through. Transfer the spinach to a shallow baking dish and arrange the egg halves on top in a single layer.

5. Pour the sauce over the eggs, sprinkle with the remaining cheese and place under the broiler until golden and bubbling.

POTATO AND RED PEPPER FRITTATA

Fresh herbs make all the difference in this simple but delicious recipe.

Preparation time 4 minutes
Cooking time 20–25 minutes

SERVES 3–4
1 pound small new potatoes,
    scrubbed
6 eggs
2 tablespoons chopped fresh mint
2 tablespoons olive oil
1 onion, chopped
2 garlic cloves, crushed
2 red bell peppers, seeded and
    roughly chopped
salt and ground black pepper
fresh mint sprigs, to garnish

1 Bring a saucepan of lightly salted water to a boil and cook the potatoes for 15–20 minutes, until just tender. Drain and cool briefly, then slice thickly.

2 Whisk the eggs and mint in a bowl. Season to taste.

3 Heat the oil in a large frying pan. Sauté the onion, garlic, peppers and potatoes for 5 minutes.

4 Pour the egg mixture over the vegetables and stir gently.

5 As it cooks, push the cooked mixture into the center so the uncooked egg runs onto the bottom.

6 When the egg mixture is just set, place the pan under a hot broiler for 2–3 minutes, until golden brown. Cut into wedges and serve, garnished with sprigs of mint.

POTATO CAKES WITH GOAT CHEESE

Preparation time 8–10 minutes
Cooking time 15–20 minutes

SERVES 2–4
1 pound potatoes
2 teaspoons chopped fresh thyme
1 garlic clove, crushed
2 scallions, chopped
2 tablespoons olive oil
4 tablespoons butter
2½ ounces firm goat cheese
salt and ground black pepper
salad greens, such as curly chicory,
   radicchio and mâche, tossed in
   walnut dressing, to serve
fresh thyme sprigs, to garnish

1 Peel and coarsely grate the
   potatoes. Using your hands,
squeeze out all the excess moisture,
then carefully combine with the
chopped thyme, garlic, scallions and
seasoning.

2 Heat half the oil and butter in a
   nonstick frying pan. Add two
large spoonfuls of potato mixture,
spacing them well apart, and press
firmly with a spatula. Cook for 3–4
minutes on each side, until golden.

3 Drain the potato cakes on
   paper towels and keep hot.
Make two more potato cakes in the
same way with the remaining mixture.
Meanwhile, preheat the broiler.

4 Cut the cheese in half
   horizontally and place one
half, cut side up, on each potato
cake. Broil for 2–3 minutes, until
golden. Garnish the potato cakes
with thyme sprigs and serve at once,
with the salad greens.

GARLIC BAKED TOMATOES

If you can find them, use Italian plum tomatoes, which have a warm, slightly sweet flavor. For large numbers of people you could use whole cherry tomatoes, tossed several times during cooking.

Preparation time 2 minutes
Cooking time 15–25 minutes

SERVES 4
3 tablespoons unsalted butter
1 large garlic clove, crushed
1 teaspoon finely grated orange zest
2 large beefsteak tomatoes or 4 firm
  plum tomatoes
salt and ground black pepper
shredded fresh basil leaves, to garnish

1 Soften the butter and blend with the crushed garlic, grated orange zest and seasoning. Chill for a few minutes.

2 Preheat the oven to 400°F. Cut the tomatoes in half crosswise.

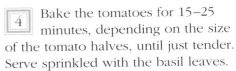

3 Place the tomatoes in an ovenproof dish and spread the butter equally over each tomato half.

4 Bake the tomatoes for 15–25 minutes, depending on the size of the tomato halves, until just tender. Serve sprinkled with the basil leaves.

COOK'S TIP
Quick cooks will find it useful to keep a supply of garlic butter in the freezer. Make it as described at left, or omit the orange rind and add chopped fresh parsley. Freeze in thick slices or chunks ready to use, or roll into a sausage shape and wrap in foil, then cut into slices when partly thawed. Wrap garlic butter very well to prevent it from imparting its odor to other foods.

LEMON CARROT SALAD

Nothing could be quicker or easier than this tangy, colorful and refreshing salad. You can grate the carrots by hand, but a food processor with a grater will be even faster and more efficient.

Preparation time 25–30 minutes
Cooking time None

SERVES 4–6
1 pound small, young carrots
grated zest and juice of ½ lemon
1 tablespoon light brown sugar
¼ cup sunflower oil
1 teaspoon hazelnut or sesame oil
1 teaspoon chopped fresh oregano, or
  pinch of dried oregano
salt and ground black pepper

1 Finely grate the carrots and place them in a large bowl. Stir in the lemon zest, 1–2 tablespoons of the lemon juice, the sugar, sunflower and hazelnut or sesame oils, and mix well.

2 Add more lemon juice and seasoning to taste, sprinkle on the oregano, toss and set aside the salad for 20 minutes before serving.

COOK'S TIP
Other root vegetables could be used in this salad. For instance, you could try replacing half the carrot with rutabaga, or use celeriac or kohlrabi instead.

MUSHROOM AND OKRA CURRY WITH MANGO RELISH

Preparation time 10 minutes
Cooking time 12–18 minutes

SERVES 4

4 garlic cloves, roughly chopped
1-inch piece of fresh ginger root,
* peeled and roughly chopped*
1–2 red chiles, seeded and chopped
³/₄ cup cold water
1 tablespoon sunflower oil
1 teaspoon coriander seeds
1 teaspoon cumin seeds
1 teaspoon ground cumin
seeds from 2 green cardamom
* pods, ground*
pinch of ground turmeric
14-ounce can chopped tomatoes
4 cups mushrooms, quartered
* if large*
8 ounces okra, trimmed and sliced
2 tablespoons chopped cilantro
basmati rice, to serve

For the mango relish
1 large ripe mango, about 1¹/₄ pounds
1 small garlic clove, crushed
1 onion, finely chopped
2 teaspoons grated fresh ginger root
1 fresh red chile, seeded and finely
* chopped*
pinch each of salt and sugar

1 For the mango relish, peel the mango and chop the flesh.

2 In a bowl, mash the mango flesh with a fork and mix in the rest of the relish ingredients. Set aside.

3 Put the garlic, ginger, chiles and 3 tablespoons of the water in a blender or food processor and blend until smooth.

4 Heat the sunflower oil in a large pan. Add the whole coriander and cumin seeds and allow them to sizzle for a few seconds. Add the ground cumin, ground cardamom and turmeric and cook for 1 minute more, until aromatic.

5 Add the garlic paste from the blender or food processor, the tomatoes, remaining water, mushrooms and okra. Stir to mix well and bring to a boil. Reduce the heat, cover, and simmer the mixture for 5 minutes.

6 Remove the cover, turn up the heat slightly and cook for another 5–10 minutes, until the okra is tender. Stir in the cilantro and serve with rice and the mango relish.

LEEK AND CARAWAY GRATIN WITH A CARROT CRUST

Tender leeks are mixed with a creamy caraway sauce and a crunchy carrot topping to make a simply superb supper.

Preparation and cooking time 28–30 minutes

SERVES 4–6

1½ pounds leeks, cut into 3-inch pieces

⅔ cup vegetable stock or water

3 tablespoons dry white wine

1 teaspoon caraway seeds

pinch of salt

1¼ cups milk, as required

2 tablespoons butter

¼ cup all-purpose flour

For the topping

2 cups fresh whole-wheat bread crumbs

1 cup grated carrot

2 tablespoons chopped fresh parsley

3 ounces Jarlsberg cheese, coarsely grated

2 tablespoons slivered almonds

1 | Place the leeks in a large pan. Add the stock or water, wine, caraway seeds and salt. Bring to a simmer, cover and cook for about 5 minutes, until the leeks are just tender.

2 | With a slotted spoon, transfer the leeks to an ovenproof dish. Reduce the remaining liquid by one-half, then add milk until you have 1½ cups.

3 | Preheat the oven to 375°F. Melt the butter in a saucepan, stir in the flour and cook, without allowing it to color, for 1 minute. Gradually add the stock and milk, stirring well after each addition, until the sauce boils and thickens. Pour the creamy sauce over the leeks in the dish and level the surface.

4 | Mix all the topping ingredients together in a bowl and sprinkle over the leeks. Bake in the oven for 15 minutes, until golden.

TAGLIATELLE WITH SPRING VEGETABLE SAUCE

A creamy pea sauce makes a wonderful combination with the crunchy young vegetables.

Preparation time 4 minutes
Cooking time 22 minutes

SERVES 4
1 tablespoon olive oil
1 garlic clove, crushed
6 scallions, sliced
2 cups frozen peas, thawed
12 ounces fresh young asparagus
2 tablespoons chopped fresh sage, plus extra leaves to garnish
finely grated zest of 2 lemons
scant 2 cups vegetable stock or water
2 cups frozen fava or lima beans, thawed
1 pound fresh or dried tagliatelle
4 tablespoons plain yogurt

COOK'S TIP
Frozen peas and beans have been used here to cut down the preparation time, but the dish tastes even better if you use fresh young vegetables when in season.

1 — Heat the oil in a pan. Add the garlic and scallions and cook gently, stirring occasionally, for 2–3 minutes, until softened.

2 — Add the peas and one-third of the asparagus, with the sage, lemon zest and stock or water. Bring to a boil, reduce the heat and simmer for 10 minutes, until tender. Purée in a blender until smooth.

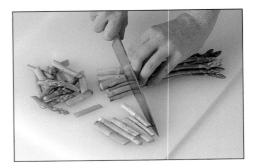

3 — Meanwhile remove the outer skins from the fava beans and discard. Set the beans aside.

4 — Cut the remaining asparagus into 2-inch lengths, trimming off any tough fibrous stems. Blanch in boiling water for 2 minutes.

5 — Cook the tagliatelle in a pan of boiling lightly salted water until just tender. Drain well.

6 — Scrape the puréed pea mixture into a pan, add the cooked asparagus and shelled beans and reheat. Stir in the yogurt. Pour the tagliatelle into a large bowl, add the sauce and toss well. Garnish with a few extra sage leaves and serve.

LEMON AND GINGER SPICY BEANS

An extremely quick, delicious meal, made with canned beans for speed.

Preparation time 6 minutes
Cooking time 17–22 minutes

SERVES 4

2-inch piece of fresh ginger root, peeled and roughly chopped
3 garlic cloves, roughly chopped
1 cup cold water
1 tablespoon sunflower oil
1 large onion, thinly sliced
1 red chile, seeded and chopped
¼ teaspoon cayenne pepper
2 teaspoons ground cumin
1 teaspoon ground coriander
½ teaspoon ground turmeric
2 tablespoons lemon juice
1½ cups chopped cilantro
14-ounce can black-eyed peas, drained and rinsed
14-ounce can aduki beans, drained and rinsed
14-ounce can navy beans, drained and rinsed
ground black pepper
crusty bread, to serve

1 Place the ginger, garlic and ¼ cup of the cold water in a blender; blend until smooth.

2 Heat the oil in a pan. Add the onion and chile and cook gently for 5 minutes, until softened. Add the cayenne pepper, cumin, coriander and turmeric and stir-fry for 1 minute.

3 Stir in the ginger and garlic paste from the blender and cook for another minute.

4 Add the remaining water, lemon juice and chopped cilantro, stir well and bring to a boil. Cover the pan tightly, lower the heat and cook for 5 minutes.

5 Add all the peas and beans to the pan and cook for 5–10 minutes more. Season with pepper and serve with crusty bread.

PIZZA MARINARA

The combination of garlic, good-quality olive oil and fresh oregano gives this pizza an unmistakably Italian flavor.

Preparation time 5 minutes
Cooking time 20–25 minutes

SERVES 2–3

4 tablespoons olive oil
1½ pounds plum tomatoes, peeled, seeded and chopped
1 pizza crust, about 10–12 inches in diameter
4 garlic cloves, cut into slivers
1 tablespoon chopped fresh oregano
salt and ground black pepper

1 Preheat the oven to 425°F. Heat about 2 tablespoons of the oil in a pan. Add the tomatoes and cook for 5 minutes, until soft.

2 Transfer the tomatoes to a sieve and let drain for about 5 minutes.

3 Place the tomatoes in a food processor or blender and purée until smooth.

4 Brush the pizza crust with half the remaining oil. Spoon the tomatoes over it and sprinkle with garlic and oregano. Drizzle with the remaining oil and season with salt and a generous grinding of black pepper. Bake for 15–20 minutes, until crisp and golden. Serve immediately.

PIZZA MARGHERITA

This classic pizza is simple to prepare. Sun-ripe tomatoes, basil and mozzarella make a good team.

Preparation time 2–3 minutes
Cooking time 15–20 minutes

SERVES 2–3
1 pizza crust, about 10–12 inches in diameter
2 tablespoons olive oil
1 cup chunky tomato sauce
5 ounces mozzarella cheese
2 ripe tomatoes, thinly sliced
6–8 fresh basil leaves
2 tablespoons freshly grated Parmesan cheese
ground black pepper

1   Preheat the oven to 425°F. Brush the pizza crust with 1 tablespoon of the oil and then spread the tomato sauce over the crust, taking it to the edges.

2   Cut the mozzarella cheese into thin slices.

3   Arrange the sliced mozzarella and tomatoes on top of the pizza crust. They look very attractive in concentric circles, with alternate slices of tomato and cheese.

4   Roughly tear the basil leaves, add and sprinkle with the Parmesan. Drizzle with the remaining oil and season with black pepper. Bake for 15–20 minutes, until crisp and golden. Serve immediately.

CHERRY PANCAKES

Pancakes provide the perfect answer to the question of what to serve for dessert when there's very little time. The ingredients are all pantry basics, even the fruit.

Preparation time 4 minutes
Cooking time 18 minutes

SERVES 4
½ cup all-purpose flour
½ cup whole-wheat flour
pinch of salt
1 egg, beaten
⅔ cup milk
⅔ cup water
a little oil for frying
For the filling
15-ounce can black cherries in juice
1½ teaspoons arrowroot
heavy cream, crème fraîche or strained plain yogurt, to serve

1   Sift the flours and salt into a bowl, adding any bran left in the sieve to the bowl at the end.

COOK'S TIPS
If fresh cherries are in season, cook them gently in enough apple juice just to cover them, and then thicken the juice with arrowroot as in Step 5.

The basic pancakes will freeze very successfully. Interleave them with nonstick paper or wrap them in plastic wrap and seal. Freeze for up to six months. Thaw at room temperature.

2   Make a well in the center of the flour and add the beaten egg. Gradually beat in the milk and water, whisking hard until all the liquid is incorporated and the batter is smooth and bubbly.

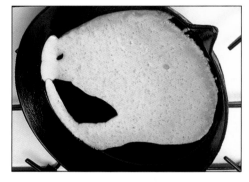

3   Heat a small nonstick frying pan with a small amount of oil until the pan is very hot. Pour in just enough batter to cover the bottom of the pan, swirling the pan to cover the bottom evenly.

4   Cook until the pancake is set and golden, and then turn to cook the other side. Slide onto a paper towel; make seven more pancakes.

5   Drain the cherries, reserving the juice. Blend about 2 tablespoons of the juice from the can of cherries with the arrowroot in a saucepan. Stir in the rest of the juice. Heat gently, stirring, until boiling.

6   Stir the mixture over medium heat for about 2 minutes, until it thickens and clears. Add the cherries and stir until thoroughly heated. Spoon the cherries into the pancakes and fold them in quarters. Serve at once, with heavy cream, crème fraîche or strained plain yogurt, if you like.

NECTARINE–PUFF PASTRY TARTS

These delicious, yet simple, fresh fruit pastries are easy to put together, but the puff pastry makes them seem very elegant.

Preparation time 15 minutes
Cooking time 12–15 minutes

SERVES 6
8 ounces frozen puff pastry, thawed
1 pound nectarines
1 tablespoon butter
2 tablespoons sugar
freshly grated nutmeg
crème fraîche or lightly whipped
  cream, to serve (optional)

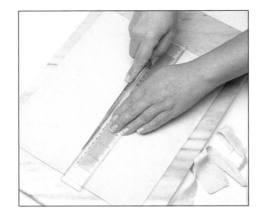

1 Lightly butter a large baking sheet and sprinkle very lightly with water.

2 On a lightly floured surface, roll out the puff pastry to a large rectangle, about 16 × 10 inches, and cut into six smaller rectangles.

COOK'S TIP
Use ready-rolled puff pastry for speed.

3 Transfer to the baking sheet. Using the back of a small knife, scallop the edges of the pastry. Then, using the tip of the knife, score a line ½ inch from the edge of each rectangle to form a border. Preheat the oven to 400°F.

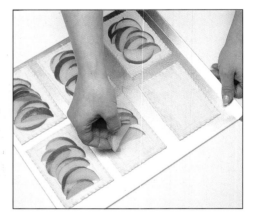

4 Cut the nectarines in half and remove the pits, then slice the fruit thinly. Arrange the nectarine slices down the center of the rectangles, leaving the borders on each uncovered. Sprinkle the fruit with the sugar and a little nutmeg.

5 Bake for 12–15 minutes, until the edges of the pastry are puffed and the fruit is tender. Transfer the tarts to a wire rack to cool slightly. Serve warm with a little crème fraîche or lightly whipped cream, if you like.

MEXICAN FRITTERS

Preparation time 15 minutes
Cooking time 12–15 minutes

SERVES 6
2 cups all-purpose flour
1 teaspoon baking powder
½ teaspoon salt
1 tablespoon granulated sugar
1 egg, beaten
½ cup milk
2 tablespoons butter, melted
oil, for frying
sugar for dusting
For the syrup
1⅓ cups light brown sugar
3 cups water
1 inch cinnamon stick
1 clove

1 Make the syrup. Combine all the ingredients in a saucepan. Heat, stirring, until the brown sugar has dissolved, then simmer until the mixture has reduced to a light syrup. Discard the spices. Keep the syrup warm while you make the fritters.

2 Sift the flour, baking powder and salt. Stir in the granulated sugar. Whisk the egg and the milk together. Gradually stir in the dry mixture. Beat in the butter to make a soft dough.

3 Turn out the dough onto a lightly floured board and knead until it is smooth and elastic. Divide the dough into 18 even-size pieces. Shape into balls, then flatten to disk shapes about ¾ inch thick.

4 Use the floured handle of a wooden spoon to poke a hole through the center of each fritter. Pour oil into a deep frying pan to a depth of 2 inches. Alternatively, use a deep-fryer. Heat the oil to 375°F, or until a small cube of day-old bread added to the oil turns golden brown in 30–60 seconds.

5 Fry the fritters in batches, taking care not to overcrowd the pan, until they are puffy and golden brown on both sides. Lift out with a slotted spoon and drain on paper towels.

6 Dust the fritters with sugar and serve with the syrup.

COOK'S TIP
If you remember, make the syrup ahead of time, chilling it until needed, then warming it through quickly at the same time as you fry the fritters.

BLUEBERRY AND ORANGE CREPE BASKETS

Impress your guests with these pretty fruit-filled crêpes. When blueberries are out of season, replace them with other soft fruit, such as raspberries or strawberries.

Preparation time 5 minutes
Cooking time 15–25 minutes

SERVES 6
1¼ cups all-purpose flour
pinch of salt
2 egg whites
scant 1 cup milk
⅔ cup orange juice
strained plain yogurt, crème fraîche, or whipped cream, to serve
For the filling
4 medium oranges
8 ounces (2 cups) blueberries

[1] Preheat the oven to 400°F. To make the pancakes, sift the flour and salt into a bowl. Make a well in the center of the flour and add the egg whites, milk and orange juice. Whisk hard until all the liquid has been incorporated and the batter is smooth and bubbly. Pour it into a measuring cup.

COOK'S TIPS
You'll need to work quickly to make this dessert in half an hour. If you can, make the batter ahead of time: It will improve on standing. Stir it before cooking the pancakes. Fill the pancake baskets seconds before serving, or they will absorb the fruit juice and start to soften.

[2] Lightly grease a heavy or nonstick frying pan and heat it until it is very hot. Pour in just enough batter to cover the bottom of the pan, swirling it to cover the bottom of the pan evenly.

[3] Cook for 1–2 minutes, until the pancake has set and is brown underneath, then turn it to cook the other side. Slide the pancake onto a sheet of paper towel, and then cook the rest of the batter, to make at least six pancakes in all.

[4] Place six small ovenproof bowls or molds on a baking sheet and drape the pancakes over them. Bake them for about 10 minutes, until they are crisp and set into shape. Carefully lift the "baskets" from the molds.

[5] Meanwhile, pare a thin piece of orange zest from one orange and cut it into fine strips. Blanch the strips in boiling water for 30 seconds, rinse them in cold water, drain them and set them aside.

[6] Cut the peel and pith from all the oranges. Divide the oranges into segments, catching the juice in a pan. Add the orange segments and blueberries to the pan and warm the mixture gently. Spoon the fruit into the baskets and sprinkle the shreds of zest over the top. Serve immediately with yogurt, crème fraîche or cream.

BAKED PEACHES WITH A CORNFLAKE TOPPING

Make this simple family dessert in minutes, using familiar pantry ingredients.

Preparation time 2 minutes
Cooking time 20 minutes

SERVES 4

14-ounce can peach slices
    in juice
2 tablespoons golden raisins
1 cinnamon stick
strip of fresh orange zest
2 tablespoons butter
1½ cups cornflakes
1 tablespoon sesame seeds

1 Preheat the oven to 400°F. Drain the canned peach slices, reserving the juice, and then arrange them in a shallow ovenproof dish.

2 Place the peach juice, raisins, cinnamon stick and orange zest in a pan and bring to a boil. Lower the heat and simmer for 3–4 minutes, to reduce the liquid by about half. Remove the cinnamon stick and orange zest and spoon the syrup over the peaches.

3 Melt the butter in a small pan and stir in the cornflakes and sesame seeds.

4 Spread the cornflake mixture over the fruit. Bake for about 15 minutes, or until the topping is crisp and golden. Serve hot.

SUMMER BERRY SPONGE TART

When soft fruits are in season, try making this delicious sponge tart. Serve warm from the oven with scoops of vanilla ice cream.

Preparation time 10 minutes
Cooking time 15 minutes

SERVES 4–6

softened butter, for greasing
1 pound (4 cups) soft fruit, such as raspberries, blackberries, black currants, red currants, strawberries or blueberries
2 eggs, at room temperature
about ¼ cup sugar
1 tablespoon all-purpose flour
½ cup ground almonds or hazelnuts
vanilla ice cream, to serve

1 Preheat the oven to 375°F. Brush a 9-inch tart pan with softened butter and line the bottom with a circle of baking parchment. Place the fruit in the bottom of the pan, adding a little sugar if the fruit is tart.

COOK'S TIPS

When time is short (or the soft fruit season has passed) use frozen fruits, but make sure they are thawed and well drained before use. To continue the almond theme, you could decorate the tart just before serving with a sprinkling of toasted almonds.

2 Whisk the eggs and sugar together for 3–4 minutes, or until the whisk leaves a thick trail across the surface. Combine the flour and almonds or hazelnuts, then fold into the egg mixture with a spatula, retaining as much air as possible.

3 Spread the mixture on top of the fruit. Bake for about 15 minutes, or until the sponge has set. Remove the tart from the pan and transfer to a serving plate. Serve warm with vanilla ice cream.

FRUITY RICOTTA CREAMS

Ricotta is an Italian soft cheese with a smooth texture and a mild, slightly sweet flavor. Served here with candied fruit peel and delicious chocolate—it is quite irresistible.

Preparation time 25 minutes
Cooking time None

SERVES 4

1½ cups ricotta
2–3 tablespoons Cointreau or other
    orange liqueur
2 teaspoons grated lemon zest
2 tablespoons confectioners' sugar
⅔ cup heavy cream
5 ounces candied peel, such as
    orange, lemon and citron,
    finely chopped
2 ounces semisweet chocolate,
    finely chopped
chocolate curls, to decorate
amaretti biscuits, to serve (optional)

1 Using the back of a wooden spoon, push the ricotta through a fine sieve into a large bowl.

2 Add the liqueur, lemon zest and sugar and beat well until the mixture is light and smooth.

3 Whip the cream in a large bowl until it forms soft peaks.

4 Gently fold the cream into the ricotta mixture with the candied peel and chopped chocolate.

5 Spoon the mixture into four glass serving dishes and chill until ready to serve. Decorate with chocolate curls and serve with amaretti biscuits, if you like.

HOT FRUIT WITH MAPLE BUTTER

Preparation time 20 minutes
Cooking time 10 minutes

SERVES 4

1 large papaya, halved
2 bananas
8 tablespoons (1 stick) butter, diced
¼ cup pure maple syrup
1 large mango, peeled and sliced
1 small pineapple, peeled and cubed

1 Scoop out the seeds from the papaya, slice and peel.

2 Peel the bananas, then cut them in half lengthwise.

3 Put the butter and maple syrup in a food processor and blend until smooth and creamy, scraping down the sides of the processor bowl once or twice if necessary. Scrape the maple butter into a bowl and set it aside. (You can also use a handheld blender for the job, and you'll only need one bowl.)

4 Mix the bananas and papaya in a gratin dish, cutting the papaya slices into chunks if you prefer. Add the mango and pineapple and mix gently. Preheat the broiler.

5 Broil the fruit under medium heat for 10 minutes, or until tender, turning it occasionally and brushing it frequently with the maple butter.

6 Arrange the fruit on a warmed serving platter and dot with the remaining maple butter. Sprinkle with a little ground cinnamon, if you like, and serve the fruit piping hot.

COOK'S TIP
Be sure to use pure maple syrup, as imitations have little of the taste of the real thing.

CREPES SUZETTE WITH COINTREAU AND COGNAC

Thin pancakes filled with Cointreau-flavored butter and flambéed with Cognac may be a classic, but they remain as popular as ever.

Preparation time 8–10 minutes
Cooking time 14 minutes

SERVES 6
1 cup all-purpose flour
1/2 teaspoon salt
2 eggs, beaten
cups milk
oil, for frying
juice of 2 oranges
3 tablespoons Cognac
confectioners' sugar, for dusting
strips of thinly pared orange zest,
    to decorate

For the orange butter
12 tablespoons (1 1/2 sticks) unsalted
    butter
1/4 cup granulated sugar
grated rind of 2 oranges
2 tablespoons Cointreau

1. Make the orange butter. Cream the butter with the sugar, orange zest and Cointreau. Set aside while you make the pancake batter.

2. Sift the flour and salt into a bowl, make a well in the center and beat in the eggs. Gradually stir in the milk and beat to a smooth batter. Pour into a measuring cup. Heat the oil in a pan, pour in a little batter and make a thin pancake. Cook until the underside is golden, turn over and cook the other side. Slide out of the pan. Make at least five more pancakes.

3. Spread the pancakes with half the orange butter and fold into neat quarters.

4. Heat the rest of the orange butter in a frying pan with the orange juice, add all the folded pancakes and turn them carefully to heat them through. Push the pancakes to one side of the pan and pour in the Cognac. Heat, then carefully set alight. When the flames die down, spoon the sauce over the pancakes. Serve immediately, dusted with confectioners' sugar and decorated with strips of orange zest.

COOK'S TIP
Not traditional, but equally delicious, is to use rum in place of the Cointreau and Cognac, and add sliced fresh pineapple and a little toasted coconut.

CHOCOLATE SOUFFLES

These soufflés are easy to make and can be prepared in advance if you can spare the time—the filled dishes can wait for up to one hour before baking. Use good-quality chocolate.

Preparation time 10 minutes
Cooking time 18–20 minutes

SERVES 6

6 ounces semisweet chocolate, chopped
10 tablespoons unsalted butter, cut
* into small pieces*
4 large eggs, separated
2 tablespoons orange liqueur
* (optional)*
¼ teaspoon cream of tartar
3 tablespoons granulated sugar
confectioners' sugar, for dusting
For the white chocolate sauce
6 tablespoons whipping cream
3 ounces white chocolate, chopped
1–2 tablespoons orange liqueur
grated zest of ½ orange

1 Generously butter six ⅔-cup ramekins. Sprinkle each with a little sugar and tap out any excess. Put the ramekins on a baking sheet.

2 In a heavy saucepan over very low heat, melt the chocolate and butter, stirring until smooth. Remove from the heat and cool slightly, then beat in the egg yolks and orange liqueur, if using. Set aside, stir occasionally.

3 Preheat the oven to 425°F. In a clean grease-free bowl, beat the egg whites slowly until frothy. Add the cream of tartar, increase the speed and beat until they form soft peaks. Gradually sprinkle in the sugar, 1 tablespoon at a time, beating until the whites are stiff and glossy.

4 Stir a third of the whites into the cooled chocolate mixture to lighten it, then pour the chocolate mixture over the remaining whites. Using a rubber spatula or large metal spoon, gently fold the sauce into the whites. (Don't worry about a few white streaks.) Spoon into the prepared dishes and put them back on the baking sheet. Bake for 10–12 minutes, until well risen.

5 Meanwhile, make the white chocolate sauce. Put the chocolate and cream in a small saucepan. Stir over low heat until melted and smooth. Remove from the heat and stir in the liqueur and orange zest, then pour into a pitcher. Serve the soufflés as soon as they are cooked, dusted with confectioners' sugar and accompanied by the sauce.

AMARETTO SOUFFLE

Preparation and cooking time 30 minutes

SERVES 6

7 tablespoons sugar
6 amaretti biscuits, coarsely crushed
6 tablespoons Amaretto liqueur
4 eggs, separated, plus 1 egg white
2 tablespoons all-purpose flour
1 cup milk
pinch of cream of tartar (if needed)
confectioners' sugar, for dusting

1 Preheat the oven to 400°F. Thoroughly butter a 6¼-cup soufflé dish and sprinkle it with a little of the sugar.

2 Put the crushed amaretti biscuits in a bowl. Sprinkle them with 2 tablespoons of the Amaretto liqueur and set aside while you make the soufflé base.

3 Mix the egg yolks, flour and 2 tablespoons of the sugar.

4 Heat the milk in a heavy pan. When it is almost boiling, stir it into the egg mixture.

5 Pour the mixture back into the pan. Set over low heat and simmer gently for 3–4 minutes, or until thickened, stirring occasionally. Remove from the heat and gradually add the remaining Amaretto liqueur, stirring all the time.

6 In a grease-free bowl, beat the 5 egg whites until they will hold soft peaks. (If not using a copper bowl, add the cream of tartar as soon as the whites are frothy.) Add the remaining sugar and continue beating until stiff.

7 Add about one-quarter of the whites to the liqueur mixture and stir in with a rubber spatula. Add the remaining whites and fold in gently.

8 Spoon half of the mixture into the prepared soufflé dish. Cover with a layer of the moistened amaretti biscuits, then spoon the remaining soufflé mixture on top.

9 Bake for 20 minutes, or until the soufflé is risen and lightly browned. Sprinkle with sifted confectioners' sugar and serve.

COOK'S TIP

Some people like soufflés to be completely cooked. Others prefer a soft, creamy center. The choice is up to you. To check how cooked the middle is, insert a thin skewer into the center: it will come out almost clean or with some moist particles clinging to it.

CINNAMON AND APRICOT SOUFFLES

Don't expect this to be difficult simply because it's a soufflé—it really couldn't be easier.

Preparation time 15 minutes
Cooking time 12–15 minutes

SERVES 4
flour, for dusting
3 eggs
½ cup apricot fruit spread
finely grated zest of ½ lemon
1 teaspoon ground cinnamon, plus
   extra to decorate

1 Preheat the oven to 375°F. Lightly grease four individual soufflé dishes and dust them lightly with flour.

2 Separate the eggs, placing the yolks in one bowl and the whites in a second, grease-free bowl. Add the apricot fruit spread, grated lemon zest and cinnamon to the egg yolks.

3 Using a handheld electric mixer, beat the egg yolk mixture hard until it is thick and pale in color. Beat the egg whites with clean beaters until they are stiff enough to hold soft peaks.

4 Using a metal spoon or spatula, fold the egg whites evenly into the yolk mixture. Spoon into the prepared dishes. Bake the soufflés for 12–15 minutes, until well risen and lightly browned. Serve at once.

INDEX

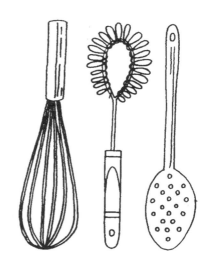

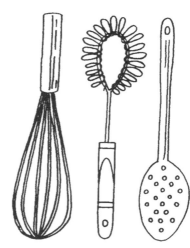